LOOKING BACK AT
LAYERTHORPE
A YORK SUBURB

by
Avril E. Webster

ISBN 1 85853 022 9

Published by
QED BOOKS
1 Straylands Grove, York, England, YO3 0EB
Telephone/Facsimile 01904 424381

Printed by
J. W. Bullivant & Son
296 Bishopthorpe Road, York, YO2 1LG
Telephone 01904 623241 Facsimile 01904 621670

CONTENTS

Outside Cover: *Premises of J. H. Walker, builders and coal merchants,*
                Layerthorpe Bridge. 1928.

Inside Cover: *Reproduced from the 1909 Ordnance Survey Map.*
                © Crown Copyright.

FOREWORD

For me, Layerthorpe is a distant memory, a district through which I cycled during the 1940s on my way to school. All I can recall is the closely built terraced housing overshadowed by a large gasometer. It seemed a very ordinary piece of the York landscape.

I now see that Layerthorpe as it was then represented a type of working-class neighbourhood that has been taken for granted for too long. As an academic urban historian I have found that studying the history of such districts can tell us much about urban development and how poorer people in the city lived and worked in the past. I welcome this publication by my sister therefore for professional as well as for personal reasons. It seems to me increasingly urgent for local historians to recover the history of these older urban neighbourhoods as many no longer exist, having been replaced either by new housing developments or, as in the case of Layerthorpe, by industrial estates.

For Avril the writing of this history has been a labour of love. It has occupied her time for several years and involved much searching through documentary records and the interviewing of older residents. From these sources she describes the origins of Layerthorpe and the developments affecting it in the 19th and 20th centuries. She provides details of the people who lived there and of their housing conditions, workplaces, shops and local institutions with some intriguing glimpses of a street and pub culture that no longer survives. The photographs and individual reminiscences which illustrate this local history also help in rekindling our perceptions of the sort of neighbourhood that 'old' Layerthorpe used to be.

Dr. David A Reeder.
Senior Research Associate
at the Centre for Urban History (Leicester University)
Educated: Nunthorpe Grammar School. (Head Boy 1948 - 49).

INTRODUCTION

The idea of a book on the history of Layerthorpe was brought about by talking to my father in law, Mr. Ernest Webster, about life in that area in the early part of this century. He gave me some old family photographs and told me many interesting, some sad, some funny anecdotes and incidents that he remembered from his youth in Layerthorpe. Since then, most of the houses and shops have been demolished, the whole area around Foss Bank altered and the families, characters and stories may have been lost forever. I set myself the task of not only recalling those days but trying to trace the development of this area from its beginnings in Viking times to the present day. As far as possible the material has been organised in chronological order, but where appropriate certain topics have been brought up to date.

In the process of my research, I met many interesting and interested people who enjoyed recalling the old days in Layerthorpe. Obviously I could not mention every individual family and I sincerely apologise to anyone who thinks their family should have had a mention. So I dedicate this book to all those people who have ever lived or worked or had any connection with Layerthorpe, and especially my father in law who will be ninety six this year, but whose tales will live on for ever.

ACKNOWLEDGEMENTS

My thanks go to all those who have helped me with this work. To my son David and daughter Ann who had the task in translating my terrible hand writing and spent many hours slaving away over the word processor. To all my family, and Cliff, for all their encouragement, patience and understanding. To all the staff at York City Archives, the Borthwick Institute For Historical Research and York Reference Library. To Mr. David Poole for all his help and information, to Miss Pauline Coldrick for the article on St. Cuthbert's Church and to Mrs. Jennifer Kaner for all her help and encouragement. Grateful thanks also to all those former Layerthorpe residents who have loaned photographs and given valuable information and to all who have helped in any way to make this publication possible.

Early Times

This is the story of the area that lies between Peasholme Green and Heworth known as Layerthorpe. Tracing its development from a small village, through to the busy thriving community that existed in the working class housing of the 19th. and 20th. century to the industrial estate of today. The name Layerthorpe is of Viking or Scandinavian origin, thorpe meaning a settlement. Layer could be from Leger meaning a burial place, or Laira, Leira meaning a clayey place.[1]

Before there was a bridge over the Foss, the river was crossed at that point by a ford, lair ford or clay ford. In Anglo Saxon times the area was also known as Larethorp, Leirthorp or Legathorpe. Its position on the left bank of the Foss suggests it could also have been a commercial settlement. We do know that the Foss was used more commercially in earlier times than now. Evidence of Roman wharves have been found at Hungate, and remains of pottery kilns at Peasholme. Roman coffins were also found near the main Layerthorpe road that led to Heworth, near the site of the old St. Mary's church in 1855.

The King's Fish Pool

After the Norman Conquest, King William 1st. dammed the River Foss just below his new castle in order to secure an adequate supply of water, destroying a carucate of land and two mills. This stretch of water became known as the King's or Royal fish pond. It stretched from Castle Mills to Layerthorpe Bridge reaching out to Tang Hall fields and as far as the Abbey Mills along Huntington Road. This pond or lake acted as a natural defence for the city and the stretch from Layerthorpe Postern to the Red Tower on Foss Islands was never defended by the city's walls. Along the west bank of the Foss lay the area known as the Marsh.[2]

There were three landing places on the fishpond, one at Layerthorpe Bridge, one at St. Margaret's landing just below St. Margaret's church, and the third at the Carmelite Friary in Hungate. Royal permission had to be granted to cross the pond. Keepers were appointed by the King to look after and sell the fish and generally see to the pond's upkeep, and repairs to the Foss bank and dam. At sometime the pond was allowed to decay and in the 17th. century documents reveal that it was shrinking in size and gradually silting up to form marshy islands.[3]

The fishing rights to the Foss were held by the Meynell Ingram family until the 1850s when they were purchased by York Corporation. They also bought out the Foss Navigation Company at this time and began work on drainage, sewerage and filling in the low-lying Foss Islands area and making Foss Islands Road. The area occupied by the King's fishpond is still known today as the Foss Islands.[4]

St. Mary's Church and burial ground

On rising ground, fifty yards from the River Foss, on the south east side of the road to Heworth, was in medieval times a small church and burial ground dedicated to St. Mary. It was probably there in 1184 when Rainbald priest of Leirthorpe was witness to a charter. In the Archbishop's Visitation of Layerthorpe in 1409, the parishioners said they lacked a missal (prayer book) and were too poor to buy one, Mass was only said once a week. In 1472 they reported that the nave of the church needed glass in the windows, and the cemetery walls were in a state of dilapidation. Alice, wife of John Brigham bequeathed six shillings and eight pence to buy a book for the church but he withheld the money. He also promised six pence to buy a torch for the church, but when approached refused to pay. John Barton left twelve pence to the church, but this money was withheld by Robert R. How of 'Jobertgate'!

The early inhabitants of Layerthorpe were buried in this churchyard. In 1510 Alexander Wilson of Layerthorpe asked to be buried in the chancel of this church before the image of Our Lady. The church was demolished in 1595, and the parish joined to St. Cuthbert's.[5]

In 1920, the Rev. Pyne of St. Cuthbert's, asked York Corporation if they would purchase the site of this old church and keep it as a rest garden for Layerthorpe inhabitants. Although initially the Estates Committee agreed to this proposal, the council could not agree on who would pay for the maintenance of such a garden.[6] The matter was never decided, so this site remained as a grassy area until the 1970's when it was developed, being at present part of Allied Carpets show room and car park.

Layerthorpe Bridge and Postern

Layerthorpe Postern stood at the end of Layerthorpe Bridge adjoining the city walls in Peasholme Green. It was quite unlike the other York posterns. It arched the roadway which was then quite narrow, but was wide and high enough for wagons to pass through. The roof was battlemented and it had iron bound doors. It was taken down when the road was widened in 1829.

Layerthorpe Bridge and Postern before 1829

Layerthorpe Bridge was first mentioned as early as 1200. In 1362, John de Popelton, left twelve pence for its repair and upkeep. Isobel de Donynton left her best dish but one and a large cup. In 1391 Anabilla, wife of William Holmes gave forty shillings towards its repair. In 1537 John Shaw, Mayor of York, left ten shillings for the mending of Layerthorpe Bridge. In the siege of York in 1644 the bridge was broken by the Royalists to stop the Parliamentarians, who were besieging the city from their camp in Heworth, from entering the town at that point. It was not repaired until 1656, and in the meantime planks were laid down for foot passengers.[7]

This bridge, which up to 1828 was a horse bridge, consisting of several low narrow arches. In 1815 the Foss Navigation Company took down a portion of the bridge and enlarged the centre arch, so as to admit vessels. Up to this time the bridge was always referred to in old deeds and marked on maps as Layerthorpe Brigg or Bridge or Layerthorpe Postern Bridge.

In 1829, York Corporation demolished the old bridge and postern (which was in a bad state of repair) and widened the road. A new bridge was built in stone and brick using materials from the old bridge. Mr. Peter Atkinson was the architect and the cost then was one thousand five hundred pounds. In the City Engineer's plan for this project, the new bridge was referred to as Peasholme Green Bridge.[8] However this name does not seem to have been very popular, and on the 1852 Ordnance Survey map, and on later maps and records, it is once again called Layerthorpe Bridge. It was widened again in 1924 when the work was carried out by unemployed men in a special scheme organised by York Corporation.[9]

Vicars Choral

The Vicars Choral owned land in Layerthorpe, mostly near the gas works, where Vicars Row and Vicars Terrace once stood. The Vicars Choral were a group of Vicars attached to the Dean and Chapter. They acted as deputies for the Canons of York Minster in the church services. They sang psalms and chanted masses for the souls of the dead. In medieval times everyone believed in the After Life, and thought that the more psalms that were sung for their souls after death, the better time they would have in the next world. They lived in little houses in the Bedern off Goodramgate, but ate in a communal hall, Bedern Hall. Over the years they acquired a lot of land and property in York and the surrounding area. The deeds for the sale of these lands give us a fascinating glimpse into life in medieval times in Layerthorpe and York.

The Vicars Choral also held land near Mill Lane in Heworth called Spittalcroft or Vicar's Leas and had two windmills and a tile works there in the 14th. century. They also had land near the old St. Mary's Church in Layerthorpe and some fields near Layerthorpe Bridge.[10] These closes or fields were the centre of a dispute in 1809. The new Rector of St. Cuthbert's Church in which the parish of St. Mary's was now united, demanded tithes or compensation for the same from the owner, a Mr. Hopwood, who had purchased them from a Mr. Clough and Mr. Townend in 1778. The Rector produced a book of tithes but because it could not be proved that these fields were actually the ones mentioned in his book, the case did not succeed. However the old documents did reveal that two closes and the parsonage house, situated near Layerthorpe Bridge, had been in the possession of the Dean and Chapter, and in Elizabethan times leased by a Mr. Robert Cripling.[11]

Robert Cripling

An interesting inhabitant of Layerthorpe in Elizabethan times was one Robert Cripling who was Lord Mayor of York in 1579/80. He was a bowyer, and was fined at the Quarter Sessions for taking wood and stone in a boat over the King's fish pool to build his house in Layerthorpe.[12] He was quite a rebel, and not liked by the York Corporation because he spoke his mind. He spoke out against the Minster preachers with "violent and disorderly speeches, and also uttered very unseemly and foul words." He also horrified the good York citizens by refusing to live within the city walls, and by his habit of walking gownless and alone about the streets with his walking stick over his shoulder. He also had a Catholic wife and it was said he favoured the Catholics and did not fine them enough for non attendance at church. He was finally deprived of his citizenship and thrown into prison for a time and the York Corporation were alarmed lest the Queen should think ill of them for electing "So rash and heady a man to be their chief governor".[13]

Plague in the City

In 1538 when there was a severe outbreak of plague in York, the Corporation ordered that all infected people had to be housed in certain buildings in Layerthorpe and in lodges on the Tang Hall fields. The people were to be re-housed elsewhere and Layerthorpe Postern to be closed. [1]

Chapter I. Notes and References

(1) A H Smith. *Place names of the East Riding of Yorks and York.* (1937) 292.293

(2) Raine A., *Medieval York.* J. Murray. (1955) 287

(3) Ibid. 14.

(4) M. Fife and P. Walls, *The River Foss,* W. Sessions Ltd. 1981.

(5) Raine. A. 287.288.

(6) York City Archives. (Subsequently referred to as Y.C.A.) *York Council Minutes.* (1919, 1920). 291.295.

(7) Raine A. 287

(8) Y.C.A. *Layerthorpe Bridge 1828/29* K64.

(9) Y.C.A. *Y.C. Minutes.* (1924).

(10) Yorkshire Archaeological Society. Record series vol. 148 Ed. Dr. N. Tringham (1993) *Charters of the Vicars Choral of York Minster, City of York and suburbs to 1546.* 257-74

(11) Y.C.A. *George Leeman's Deeds* AC. 22. VC.

(12) Y.C.A. F2. 13. (1560).

(13) Kightley, C. and Semlyen, R. *Lords of the City.* (1980) 9.10.

(14) Raine. A. 288.

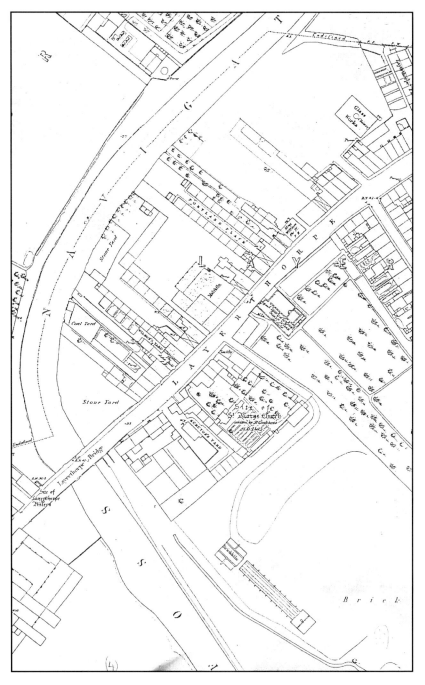

Reproduced from the 1852 Ordnance Survey Map.

CHAPTER II

Early Landowners

Layerthorpe continued as a small village with no significant changes until the 19th century. Speed's map of 1610 shows a cluster of houses, probably wooden cottages down each side of the main Layerthorpe road, with one house situated near Hallfield Lane, possibly Robert Cripling's. In the Victoria County Histories there is a mention of a Layerthorpe Hall. This belonged to Rievaulx Abbey in 1333, but after the Dissolution of the Monasteries there is no more mention of this house but the name Hallfields remains.[1] The land around Layerthorpe village was used for early brickworks, but the area near the Foss was very low-lying, and often covered by water.

Land near Layerthorpe Bridge is mentioned very early in deeds. In medieval times, John Roald priest of St. Mary's Church, held land between Eve Sywn and Alexander de Hyll and Hamo de Gaunt. The main Layerthorpe Road seemed to have been called Sunnygale.[2]

In 1660, two closes just outside Layerthorpe Postern, called Haberdasher Closes were owned by M. Jacques a Middle Temple gentleman and occupied by William Cooke, haberdasher.[3]

Principal Landowners of the 18th. and 19th. Centuries

Hallfields was a large tract of land which adjoined Layerthorpe and stretched from the Foss up to Tang Hall Bridge. It was divided into Little Hallfields and Great Hallfields. In 1711 William Rymer, a Middle Temple gentleman, sold some of his land to William Justice, gentleman of York, "Two closes, one called Lady Cripling's Close and one Watson's Close, also Bridgend Close and Bull Lane Closes for £80".[4]

This land passed to his son Henry Justice who once had lived in the Pavement. Although he was a barrister at law, Lord of the Manor of Rufforth and a man of property, he stole books and prints from Trinity College Cambridge. He was discovered, tried and convicted and sent as a common criminal to the plantations of America for seven years. On his return he took up residence in London and Belgium. He deserted his wife Elizabeth and left her and his children dependent on relatives in York. In 1734, Elizabeth decided to go to Russia as a governess and she described her travels in a book published by T. Gent of York in 1739.[5]

In 1777, William Justice, son of Henry, sold some of his land to J. Clough a builder and G. Townend a clerk of the city. This land consisted of "two closes or meadow on the south east side but not adjoining two closes, one called Little Hallfield and one called Bridgend Close". Also land near Layerthorpe Bridge containing "a messuage or dwelling house now divided into two tenements, a garden croft and bleaching yard, stable and other buildings outside Layerthorpe Postern".[6] William Justice had also sold a garden in the same area to George Earle, who died in 1777. He left a will in which he left the house he lived in to his wife Elizabeth but not the garden. "That I shall dispose of another way. She shall have all privilege to go into the garden and dry her clothes". He gave her all his money, furniture and plate but not "if she play the fool and marry again, then it shall be lawful for my son George to take from his mother all the money I have so generously given her".[7]

After the death of Elizabeth Earle, her son George inherited the land and money. He also came into possession of a garden in the same area which he leased from the Vicars Choral. "Land bounded by a close belonging to Thomas Withers on the east, on the west by a lane called Halfpenny Lane, on the north by the street, on the south by freehold land belonging to George Earle".[8] This land can be pinpointed as being near where later the Sunday school belonging to St. Cuthbert's church was built, just off the main Layerthorpe road and near Taylor's Engineering Works. Halfpenny Lane, which had previously led to the old St. Mary's church was in the same area and still called by that name in the 1890s.[9]

In the 1780s, John Clough and George Townend sold some of their land, Haberdasher Close near Layerthorpe Bridge to Jonathan Hopwood. This land eventually passed down to his son in law William Grey. In 1794, trustees of John Clough and George Townend sold most of their land on the Hallfields, which was recorded as "Two closes lying together known as Great Hallfields", for nine hundred and fifty-seven pounds to Thomas Withers, a Doctor of Medicine. John Dale, Lancelot Tasker and Robert Atkinson, all owned land on the Hallfields in 1800.[10]

Brickworks were mentioned as being on the Hallfields as early as 1809. John Morley was advertising bricks then in the York Courant.[11] When he died in 1824 he left his brickworks to his spinster sisters Elizabeth and Ann Morley. In 1836, Henry Kidd bought these brickworks and also some land in the same area that had belonged to Peter Rymer.[12]

After the death of Thomas Withers, his land on the Hallfields passed down to Oswald Allen, who was an apothecary at the York Dispensary and had married Frances Withers, daughter of Thomas, in 1793.[13] The first houses in Bilton Street and Redeness Street were built on a site owned by Oswald Allen in the 1820s. In 1846 he sold two closes on the Hallfields to Henry Bellaby, printer and bookseller, for eighteen hundred pounds. These were situated in an area, "bounded by land belonging to Dr. Simpson on the north, by land belonging to James Barber of Tang Hall and Bull Lane on the east, by Tang Hall Beck on the south and by land belonging to George and Henry Kidd and the Brick Lane on the west".[14]

Oswald Allen also sold some of his land near Layerthorpe Bridge to Robert Atkinson in 1810. He left it to his daughter Elizabeth Atkinson who had married Henry Aiken, butler of York. In 1844 this land was sold for one thousand pounds to Mary Wilson, spinster of Kegworth, John Thomas, city gentleman and William Grey the younger of York. This consisted of land and "two houses erected by John Dale, with barn, stables, outbuildings and garden occupied by John Dale and John Brown, bounded by another part of Great Hallfields on the north owned by Mr. Kidd, land belonging to S. Tuke on the south and land near Foss Islands owned by George Leeman".

In 1834 Oswald Allen had sold some of his land near the Foss to Richard Powell, bricklayer and George Leeman. In the 1850s they owned a brick and tile works in this area, George Leeman also acquired in 1860 the land and garden that had belonged to the Earle family.[15] John Earle had been left houses and premises in Layerthorpe by his father George Earle who died in 1827. "To my son John Earle, all the premises I have situated out of Layerthorpe Postern and also my right and title in the other part of the garden and house and stable now occupied by William Saville, being a leasehold from the Vicars Choral".[16] John Earle was a successful market gardener in the 1850s and won many horticultural prizes.[17]

Henry Bellaby and George Mansfield, a city councillor, bought some of George Leeman's land near the Foss, and part was bought by the North Eastern Railway Company in the 1890s.[18] Much of the land near the old railway bridge near the Heworth end was owned by the Rymer family at this time and was known as Rymers Fields well into this century.[19]

Chapter II. Notes and References

(1) P. M. Tillot. (ed) Victoria County History. *The City of York*. (1961) 499.

(2) Y.A.R.S. *Charters of the Vicars Choral*. 257-74

(3) Y.C.A. *George Leeman's Deeds*. AC. 20 2. V.C.

(4) Borthwick Institute of Historical Research. *Fridaythorpe Prebendary Papers*. CC. A.D.D.

(5) York Reference Library Pressley, I. A *York Miscellany*. 170

(6) Borthwick. *Fridaythorpe Prebendary Papers*. CC. A.D.D.

(7) Y.C.A. *Will of George Earle,* died 1777.

(8) York Minster Library. *Deeds of the Vicars Choral*. V Box V.C.7.

(9) Y.C.A. Plans for new Sunday School. Ac. 37-48. Also in York Reference Library. Plan of ground in Layerthorpe showing old Sunday School and land under lease from Sub chantry and Vicars Choral. 1890.

(10) Borthwick. *Fridaythorpe Prebendary Papers* CC. A. DD.

(11) York Reference Library (subsequently referred to as Y.R.L.) *York Courant*. 30 October 1809.

(12) Y.C.A. E97 204/B.

(13) Y.R.L. Newspaper Index. *Oswald Allen,* died 25 March, 1848

(14) Borthwick. *Fridaythorpe Prebendary Papers*. CC. A. D.D.

(15) Y.C.A. *George Leeman's Deeds*. A.C. 20 2. V.C.

(16) Y.C.A. *Will of George Earle,* died 1827.

(17) Information supplied by Mrs. J. Kaner

(18) Y.C.A. *George Leeman's Deeds* AC. 20. 2. V.C.

(19) Information supplied by Mr. E. Webster, Woolnough House.

View of Layerthorpe from the top of the gasometer, 1928. Most of these houses were demolished in the 1930s.

Courtesy of City of York Archives

CHAPTER III

Housing Development

In the 18th. century three quarters of the population of England made their living in rural areas but with the onset of the Industrial Revolution, and later by the coming of the railways many left the country to seek their fortune in the towns.

In York the population in 1831 was 22,260 but by 1901 it had risen to 77,914. New working class houses had sprung up in areas like Layerthorpe, The Groves and Leeman Road, with undesirable high population densities.

In Victorian times, houses were mostly built by speculative builders, then bought by investors, who let them to working class men. Bilton Street, Redeness Street, Duke of York Street were some of the first houses to be used in this way, between 1820 and 1830. Bilton Street, Redeness Street were rows of terrace houses built on a site laid out by Oswald Allen. Bilton Street had thirteen occupants and Redeness Street had fifteen in the 1830s street directory. The houses were mostly of two storeys but some had attics and showed a wide variety of plans and fittings. They feature in the Royal Commission Book of Historic Buildings of York as properties worth preserving. Hallfield Place was a terrace of low houses which appear in Robert Cooper's map of 1832. They had simple plastered entrances with rectangular fan lights with geometrical glazing patterns.[1]

The houses in Hallfield Road were built about 1850. There had always been a Hallfield Lane which led to a Victorian brickworks owned by the Kidd family. Kidd's Terrace was built after 1886, on land owned by this same family.[2]

In 1850, most of the houses in these streets were solidly constructed and in good repair. According to Seebohm Rowntree's survey on York on housing in the book "Poverty" published 1901, they would be classed as "the best type of working class houses. They are situated in streets of moderate width about thirty to thirty five feet. They usually have a frontage of from 15 to 17 feet. The houses have four or five rooms and a scullery. Outside the scullery is a small cemented yard with a water closet".[3]

Mrs. Collinson remembered moving into 29 Bilton Street in 1910. It had two rooms down stairs plus a scullery, two bedrooms and attic bedrooms where her brothers slept. There was a copper and water closet in the outside yard. This house was larger than most in Bilton Street. Some of the houses at the beginning of this street, housed two families, one lived at the front, one at the back and the houses were numbered accordingly 1,1a etc.[4]

Mrs. Arnold recalled some houses in Redeness Street that had small gardens and some small cottage type houses on the main thoroughfare, especially near Layerthorpe Bridge.[5] Mr. Webster remembered some very small houses in Hallfield Place and some small courts in Bilton Street with houses built around. Cross Court was a row of seven houses which joined Bilton Street to Redeness Street.[6]

The houses situated in the area between Layerthorpe main road and the Foss were mostly built before the Public Health Act or bylaws regarding width of streets and construction of buildings had come into force. Many were damp and dark and required damp proof courses. The yard surface was often unpaved and the external woodwork frequently required painting . They were often flooded by the Foss. Most of the back to back houses in Layerthorpe were o be found in this area. There were small yards like John Bull Yard and Chicory Yard where housing of an even smaller dimension were to be found.[7] Some of the houses in Layerthorpe, especially in these areas were very shut in and received little sunlight, as reports in the city council minutes show. "2-17 Layerthorpe, obstructive buildings behind the yards, one storey lean to erections used as stables, store rooms and open sheds".

Another report in the Ministry of Health Returns, states "certain buildings or sheds behind 23 Layerthorpe belonging to Mr. Routledge and occupied by T. Mellor coal merchant, that by reason of their proximity to 12-17 Back Layerthorpe Buildings and occupied by W. Dawson, W.Jackson, A. Hunter, W. Scofield, J. Chipchase, J Lynch and owned by Mr. Powell of Coney Street, stop ventilation and access of daylight, and in our opinion should be pulled down".[8]

In Sickness and in Health

In Victorian times, the sanitary conditions in Layerthorpe and indeed in York itself were far from desirable. Underground sewers and drains were few and the streets were often filthy. Dirt and water drained into the streets. Houses that were near the Foss were flooded frequently. There were many slaughter houses and stables situated amongst the poorest houses and piles of manure often accumulated in the roadways.

In 1849, the inhabitants of St. Cuthbert's parish which included Layerthorpe, wrote to the health inspector appointed to examine the sanitary conditions of York, pointing out the condition of the area. "We the inhabitants of the above parish, in vestry meeting, beg most respectfully, to invite your especial attention to the great necessity of sanitary regulations and improvements, which the health of the population of this district seems to require and to the defective condition of some of the cottage property, especially near Layerthorpe Bridge".[9]

In 1850, Mr. Alderson, surgeon to No. 4 district of the York Poor Law Union which consisted of Layerthorpe, Hungate and Peasholme Green, reported:- "The drainage of Layerthorpe is very bad at present. The drain goes in a circle on a lower level than the Foss. It had to be extended under the bridge and consequently there is a great accumulation of dust and filth in the gutters. In Portland Place, a new street built recently, fever is prevalent. The people complain of bad smells from the drainage. The prevalence of fever in the Layerthorpe district must be attributed in a great measure to the state of the drains".[10]

In 1852, Mr. Webster, a pot maker whose business, employing eight men was at the bottom of Hallfield Road, applied to the city council for planning permission to build a new house in Layerthorpe. The plans were considered but not proved. The report of the sub committee which had inspected the road and area stated that the locality was imperfectly drained, the roads were in a shocking state and in their opinion no district in York had been more shamefully treated. On one occasion a fever of a most malignant character had arisen from lack of drainage, and they urged the Board of Health to give the matter its earnest and prompt attention. The members of the Health Committee answered , "What were they to do, it would cost a lot of money to build a drain, and they were told on the one hand to drain the city and on the other keep the rates down".[11]

There were many suggestions for ways to drain Layerthorpe. One was to tunnel under the Foss and drain into the Ouse as so many drains ran into the Foss. The River Foss was a great impediment to draining Layerthorpe as long as it remained at its present level. It was suggested that locks at Castle Mills were re-sited a little above Monk Bridge and the river dredged, so as to be five feet deep and level with the Ouse. However it was not until 1855 that a sewer was built to drain Layerthorpe and Heworth.[12]

In 1849 there had been a severe epidemic of Asiatic Cholera in York which was caused by contaminated water. There were 155 burials in the York cemetery between July and October of that year. The outbreak had started in Skeldergate, but soon spread to Layerthorpe. There were 22 burials in 24 days, many being buried on the same or following day that they died. There were two cases of both a husband and wife dying on the same day.[13]

There had always been cases of scarlet fever, dysentery and other infectious diseases occurring regularly in Layerthorpe, and the York area. Children, especially the very young were particularly at risk. In the years 1874 - 1884 a 1/3rd. of all deaths in York were children under 5. Summer diarrhoea, most prevalent in hot summers, killed many babies under 1 year due to dehydration. In 1898 115 children under 5 died from diarrhoea and dysentery, 80 from bronchitis and diseases of the respiratory organs and 32 from measles.[14]

In 1884 there was a typhoid outbreak in York which affected Layerthorpe very badly. No outbreaks had approached it in severity over the previous twelve years. There were forty cases in Layerthorpe.

The reason for this outbreak was blamed on the fact that there was no systematic collection of "night soil". All was left to individual action. It had been the rule to retain the contents of the privies and ashpits for weeks on end. In many places, in the case of back to back houses, contents had to be carried through the house. Foul privies and defective sanitary arrangements about houses were common agents in retaining typhoid infection in one locality. Several people using one privy was a frequent means of spreading the disease.

On an average of more than thirty days in a year the sewers were likely to flood, extending over the whole of Hungate and Layerthorpe. The main sewer affected was the one which discharged itself at Blue Bridge and the branches which joined it from Hungate and Layerthorpe. All these conditions were aggravated in 1884, after a summer of little rain, when the sewers were not flushed. Foul and offensive gullies had been a source of complaint in nearly every part of the city that year, and the hot dry summer constituted the climatic conditions required to give rise to this infection. But all these bad conditions themselves were not enough to account for the terrific epidemic of 1884, as there had always been typhoid, diphtheria and similar diseases around. The massive spread of this disease to other areas of York in 1886 was partly blamed on a milkman of Osbaldwick. After this epidemic the Ministry of Health ordered that all new houses were to have a back lane or road, and all privies to have floors of concrete and walls of cement.[15]

After 1890 notices were sent out to owners of houses in Layerthorpe to convert their midden privies to water closets and provide clean and decent ashpits.

Excerpts from the Council Minutes in 1890

"Notices to be given to the owner of nine houses in Portland Place owned by Wm. Craven to provide four latrines and fill up the ashpits with clean dry materials. Ten houses in John Bull yard owned by W. Frankish abolish privies and ash pits and substitute five latrines".

"Wilson's yard owned by T.Pratt to provide the same, and to repair the footway near the closets and pave the passage".

1896/97

"Notice given to owner of property in Hart's Terrace. Mr Uriah Hornsey, to convert privies into water closets and repair pipes".

1897/98

"Mr. Uriah Hornsey ordered to carry out sanitary work on his premises in Hart's Terrace".

Mr. Hornsey objected to this notice, but after legal proceedings he agreed to make the repairs.

Even when water closets were installed, one often served a number of houses. Water taps were also a considerable distance from the house and in many cases six or more houses had to use one tap.

1905

"Houses without proper supply of water 1-17 Layerthorpe Buildings. 1 tap provides for 11 houses and 1 tap for 6 others".[16]

However in 1910 in York there was still 4,400 earth closets, 11,800 wash down closets and 3,000 waste water closets or duckets. Some of the duckets were still in use up to the 1960s.

Layerthorpe was situated in a low lying area, and in 1910, the death rate was 17.6 per 1,000 inhabitants as opposed to areas like Clifton and Heworth, which were in open high situations and where the death rate was 9.1. In Hungate in 1907, the death rate was 28.9, so Layerthorpe was a little healthier place to live in than that area.[17]

Overcrowding seemed to have been a problem in Layerthorpe in the early part of this century. Mr. Horwell remembered the overcrowding especially in Portland Place, where families took turns to sleep on the beds and settees.[18]

Private slaughter houses were often situated in poor and crowded areas, and in York in 1902 these numbered no less than ninety-four. After slaughtering, the blood was allowed to run into common grates next to dwelling houses. Layerthorpe had its share of slaughter houses, some licensed some not.

In 1903, the sanitary inspector had visited premises in Layerthorpe occupied by Messrs Martin and McCoughlin general dealers and found a carcass of a cow deposited there. The owners stated it had got there by mistake. These premises were not licensed as a slaughter house. Some slaughter houses were kept in a satisfactory state.

In 1912, Robert Bridges of Little Hallfield Road made application for the renewal of his licence to use premises in Little Hallfield Road as a knacker's

Residents of Wilson's Yard, 1919, showing their proximity to the gasometer.

yard, on the site now occupied by Layerthorpe Working Men's Club. Twelve inspections of these premises were made during the year and few complaints received, all the offal being removed every day. Offensive trades such as tripe boilers, fat melters, fell mongers, tanners, leather dressers, all had to be licensed.

In 1912, John Lofthouse was charged with melting fat without consent in a building situated in a coal yard behind No.3 Layerthorpe. A manure pit adjoined the said building which was only three feet from stables in which five horses were kept.[19] Mr. Webster remembered the offensive smells from the skin and hide works, of W. D. Marks and sons, which was in "Skin Yard" possibly Wilkinson's Yard. Mr. H. Winn remembered the regular infestations of flies, a common occurrence, with properties being so close to the slaughter houses.[20]

The milk supply, a great source of typhoid infection, was unsatisfactory in the early years of this century. The milk trade at this time was in the hands of a large number of dairy men, each with a few cows. They were often kept in yards behind the houses, many in unsatisfactory conditions. The fact that there was a number of small producers selling milk to one distributor caused risk of infection. Milk was often kept in stoneware bowls and tins on the counters of small provisions shops next to herrings, onions, pickles and paraffin

Even in the 1920s some cows were kept in yards behind houses in Layerthorpe. Mrs. Finch remembered her grandmother, Mrs. Milner, having cows in the yards behind her shop in Layerthorpe and also in fields down Stockton Lane. She would milk the cows in the fields, and yards, and the milk was sold at $\frac{1}{2}$d a pint. There were many stables behind the houses. Mr. Horwell kept the horses for his coal business in a yard in Bilton St.[21]

Victorian Inhabitants

Who were the first people who went to live in the new streets in Layerthorpe in the 1840s and 50s. The little we know about them can only be gleaned from records such as early street directories and the Census Enumerator's Returns. As the area around the new housing was mostly fields, we find numerous cow keepers, market gardeners and allotment holders. There was John Hart, dairyman and cow keeper, Jonathan Calvert and John Earle market gardeners, John Webster, a brown earthenware manufacturer, employing 8 men, who had his business at the bottom of Hallfield Road. Butchers, Solomon Wilkinson, John Saville and William Kidd. Coal merchants, George Scruton and William Wray. Blacksmiths Mr. Peacock and Mr. Race.

There were five publicans in the 1850s. Thomas Sawyer at the Frog Hall, T Wilson at the John Bull and William Wilkinson at the Kings Arms, being three of them. There were also, J. Ellison, J. Watson and W. Wheatley, tilers and plasterers.[22] The Kidd family figure prominently in these early Victorian records. Henry Kidd was a stonemason from Pickering, who came to Layerthorpe in the 1820s. He bought land and brickworks that had formerly belonged to the Morley family and begun his own business at the bottom of Hallfield Road. He had ten children and each boy was put into a different trade. In the 1850s he was employing fourteen men. Kidd's Terrace was built in the 1890s on land owned by this same family.[23] In the 1890s, Mr. G Pattison had his carriage works in a yard across the road from the John Bull public house. He made every type of two and four wheeled carriage, and held the gold medal for the invention of the travelling dairy van.[24]

In Bilton Street and Redeness Street in the 1840s, the poll books and street directories reveal quite a few early inhabitants listed as gentlemen residing in the new houses. In 1840s there were Robert Bollans, James Barra, Robert Walker, M. Bell, James Horley, A. Botterill, T. & A. Wilkinson and C. & T. Wilson and Mr. Thomas Hart all noted as gentlemen. There was also John Benson librarian, Cornelius Crawshaw printer and book seller. W. Pinter, Thomas Glover, blacksmiths. James Cotnam, rope maker and Andrew Bulmer a brick and tile maker. There was a brick and tile works owned by Messrs Leeman and Thomas, which was situated near the Foss to give easy transport. P. and S. Rymer had their coal business near the Foss by Layerthorpe Bridge, later to be taken over by J. H. Walker and Sons. There were several small shops down the main Layerthorpe road, Henry Little, Francis Dutton, C. Imeson, T. Smith and W. Lazenby are all listed as shopkeepers.[25]

In the 1850s, the trades of the inhabitants were very varied. There were confectioners, white smiths and bell hangers, seamstresses, shoemakers, washerwomen, stay makers, bricklayers and agricultural labourers. Some of the families in Hallfield Road and Hart's Terrace boasted a servant or two. At this time there were more people living in Bilton Street, Redeness Street, Duke of York Street than anywhere else in the area.[26]

Many of the early inhabitants owned land in Layerthorpe, on which they had a few houses built, and consequently the streets were often named after them. Wilson's Row, Wilson's Terrace named after the Wilson family, Hart's Terrace, after Mr. Thomas Hart, and Mansfield Street after George Mansfield.

Mr. Mansfield was a builder of Layerthorpe who had his business "The Atlas works" on the corner of Hart's Terrace. He was the brother in law of the famous York photographer William Hayes, whose studio was in Monkgate. Mr. Mansfield had helped to build this studio in 1902. When Mr.

Hayes moved to Hutton Le Hole in 1911, Mr. Kidd of Layerthorpe travelled out from York to put up this same studio, for which he was paid £1-4-4d with 10 shillings deducted from this sum for his meals.[27]

Bilton Street School

Bilton Street School for boys, with accommodation for 160 scholars, was opened in 1832. Its benefactor was the Reverend Jocelyn Willey of Heworth Hall.

The school log books, which are extant from the 1860s, contain interesting snippets which give us a fascinating glimpse into Victorian life. It began as a fee paying school, parents had to pay 1d or 2d a term. The following are extracts from the log books of these times.

Feb. 12 1865 Thomas Wells drowned in attempting to cross the ice near Monk Bridge. Henry Webster and George Fletcher narrowly escaped same fate.

Feb. 22 John Ridsdale went to Layerthorpe Glass works - on trial for a month (28).

Feb. 02 1872 National thanksgiving day for recovery of the Prince of Wales, the children went in procession to attend special services at Heworth church. Tea was provided by Lady Wheler.

Feb. 11 John Smith, Thos Groves, Thos Wheatley were kept in without their dinners for refusing to do some work. I sent word to their parents, who were satisfied. In the afternoon the boys did the work.

Feb. 24 Thomas Wheatley sent home for being saucy but was reinstated on making his apology.

Feb. 1873 Thomas Horsman brought to school, had been playing truant and spent his school pence.

May 11 Complaint made by one of the parents for Mr. Patterson sticking a boy.

May 15 Had to reprove Holderess for sticking a boy. Parents satisfied.

July 11 1880 Attendance low owing to the number of children attending the soup kitchen.

July 12 Charles Hammond kept at home because his parents thought he ought to have had his fees returned. I explained to his parents, that, as he had not passed in a single subject, fees were not returnable.

Obviously even though this was a fee paying school, fees were returned if pupils did well. How ever on July 15th it was noted:-

> "Mr. Hammond came to collect his son's books, convinced that we had put his child's money for his fees in our own pockets, convinced him it was the regulations".

> In August and September there were two cases of scarlet fever and two of typhoid.

> *May 30th 1882* A great number of boys had not learnt their scripture lessons and in consequence were deprived of their game of cricket.

> *Aug. 16* (*Report of H.M. Inspector*) "I am sorry to see so many of the children absent from examinations. The lads seem to be of a rather rough and unruly character but I hope on another occasion to find them in better order".

and in 1883:–

> "Boys' behaviour much better this year. Elementary subjects are taught well and boys show considerable intelligence. Reading and writing neat and good. Singing very hearty".

> Mr. Smith who was the head master for many years retired in the 1880s and Mr. J. Wales who had been his deputy took over until 1900 when Mr. Jenkinson was appointed as headmaster.[29]

Chapter III. Notes and References

(1) Royal Commission on Historical Monuments. *City of York*. Vol. IV London (1975) 82.83.

(2) Y.C.A. *Deeds of the Kidd family*. AC. 46 - 52.(1888).

(3) B. S. Rowntree. Poverty. *A study of town life*, third edition. 3rd. ed. London (1908).

(4) Information supplied by Mrs. E. Collinson, late 116 Tang Hall Lane.

(5) Information supplied by Mrs. A. Arnold, Glen Lodge Heworth.

(6) Information supplied by Mr. E. Webster, 5 Woolnough Avenue.

(7) Y.C.A. *Ministry of Health Plan*. (1920).

(8) Y.R.L. *Reports of the Ministry of Health*. (1904-5)

(9) J.Smith. *Report to the General Board of Health on the City of York*. London (1850) 4.5.

(10) Ibid. 6.

(11) Y.C.A. *York Council Minutes* (1852).

(12) Ibid. (1855).

(13) Y.C.A. *York Cemetery Records*.

(14) Y.R.L. *Reports of the York Medical Officer of Health*. (1898-1905).

(15) Y.R.L. S.W. North. *Report of the Prevalence of Typhoid Fever in York*. (1884).

(16) Y.C.A. *Y.C. Minutes*. (1890-1898) (1905).

(17) Y.R.L. Health Reports. (1907) (1910).

(18) Information supplied by Mr. J. Horwell, late Gilamour Avenue.

(19) Y.C. Minutes. (1903) (1912).

(20) Information supplied by Mr. Webster, Mr. H. Winn, late Pottery Lane.

(21) Information supplied by Mrs. Finch, 13 Elmsland Grove.

(22) Y.R.L. F.Melville & Co. *General Directory of Hull and York*. (1855).

(23) Information supplied by Mrs. Douglas. Bishopthorpe, York.

(24) Y.R.L. Kelly's Directories Ltd., *York Directory*. (1890).

(25) Y.R.L. F. White & Co. *General Directory of York*. (1846).

(26) Y.R.L. *Census Returns for St.Cuthbert's Parish*. (1851) (1861).

(27) Buchanan. T. *William Hayes 1871 - 1940*. Hutton Press. (1986) 18.

(28) There was a small glass works situated in the area near Wilson's Yard. 1850-60. This had disappeared by 1870. Y.C.A. Rate Books. (1850-1870).

(29) Y.C.A. *Bilton Street School. Log books*. (1860-1900).

CHAPTER IV

Cattle Market and Derwent Valley Railways

The Cattle Market Branch line that was established in Layerthorpe in 1877 and later the opening of the Derwent Valley light Railway made Layerthorpe important to the farming communities and gave the area a well-needed boost to its economy.

The Foss Islands branch line or Cattle Market line as it was called was a spur from the Liverpool to Scarborough line. Its main purpose was to transport the Irish stock cattle from Liverpool to the sidings at Foss Islands where the cattle were unloaded and driven to the cattle market. Until the 1970s the cattle market was situated on the site now occupied by the Barbican Centre. The animal pens were set up in Paragon Street extending up to the city walls.

Men were employed as "cow wallopers" to bring the cattle to the market from the railway sidings and also from farms in Heworth, Osbaldwick and surrounding areas. As late as 1967, there was a report in the Y.E.P. of people complaining about cattle escaping and causing damage to gardens along the route from Osbaldwick to the cattle market.

The Derwent Valley line, whose northern terminal was at the end of Hallfield Road, was officially opened on the 19th July 1913 by Lady Deramore. It ran from Layerthorpe through Osbaldwick, Murton, Dunnington, Elvington, Wheldrake, Cottingwith, Thorganby, Skipwith, North Duffield and joined up with the Selby to Market Weighton line at Cliffe Common, a distance of sixteen miles.

The Layerthorpe station consisted of one single long platform and spacious yard with sidings, various station offices, and warehouses. Agricultural produce was the main freight of the Derwent Valley line, potatoes, corn, hay, cattle cake, sugar beet and live stock, came in from surrounding farms.[1]

The regular passenger service consisted of four up and down trains per day. Attached to the coaches were the goods wagons. On market days horse drawn wagons met trains and transported the farmers and their wives with their produce to the York market. Mrs. Richardson remembered, how as a girl, she would sit on a wall near the station and watch all the comings and goings of the trains. She said on market days, there would be cattle loaded and unloaded, farmers and farmer's wives with their covered baskets of butter, eggs and other produce. Lots of bustle and activity in Layerthorpe in those days.[2] At the height of its popularity the passenger service attracted an annual patronage of close on fifty thousand travellers.

Cattle being unloaded at Foss Island's Depot. circa 1930. Photo by T. J. Hancock.

The Sentinel locomotive at Layerthorpe 1925.

After the First World War, the passenger traffic declined, mainly because of the spread of road transport. For a time, Ford rail buses were used, carrying up to thirty-six passengers, but in spite of the substantial economy in running costs, the service was withdrawn from the Derwent valley in 1926. However special excursion trains were still run. These were often used for Sunday school trips for Layerthorpe, Hungate and Heworth children. The "Bramble Express" was also very popular, these trains stopping at various points along the line where the best brambles were to be found.

Soon after the outbreak of World War Two, aerial photographs showed, that the line now over grown with weeds due to shortage of labour, was virtually invisible from the air, therefore hard to detect by enemy bombers. Tons of steel and cement were transported along the line to construct Elvington aerodrome. Later, hundreds of thousands of tons of bombs and explosives were sent along it to build up the munitions and war material dumps which were sighted on the railway and line sides in the Derwent Valley. Petrol and ammunition were stored at Murton Lane Station, and thousand of cases of tea stored at Elvington and poisonous mustard gas at Cottingworth.

When the National Railway Museum opened in York in 1977 the D.V.R. started steam train trips for rail enthusiasts which ran from Layerthorpe to Dunnington.[3]

Chicory Smith

In Victorian times and in the early part of this century there was a Chicory works in Layerthorpe, owned by a Mr. Thomas Smith. It was situated on the left hand side from the bridge, in a yard, still known as Chicory Yard, which backed onto the Foss near the John Bull public house.[4] The chicory industry was introduced into Yorkshire in 1839, (Chicory was drunk locally instead of coffee, and supposed to be the best remedy for insomnia and indigestion.) Approximately one thousand acres were under cultivation in the immediate neighbourhood of York in the 1850s. A lot was grown in the Dunnington area. It was an important item of agriculture then and a source of profit for farmers, providing employment for both sexes. The chicory was not usually dug up until early November after the potato harvest and many casual agricultural labourers were employed in the dual harvest. The quantity grown in England then equalled that grown abroad.

Chicory was the only agricultural produce subject to excise duty. The act of 1860 laid down many provisions and stipulations regarding the drying and roasting of the chicory and the collection of this duty. The dryers and roasters had to make proper entry with the office of excise, and name every warehouse, building, shop, kiln and furnace connected with the industry. The dryers had to provide accommodation for the excise officers who took possession of the keys to the kilns when the roots where half dry until they were dry enough to go to the warehouse. Drying was a slow process, so the farmers had to wait in turn for the excise men. It was said farmers in Dunnington remembered having excise men living with them for two months at a time. In the 1860s the excise duty on chicory was increased from three shillings a cwt. to twenty four shillings and three pence a cwt. Imports then increased at the expense of the home grown. A deputation of Yorkshire Chicory Manufacturers was raised at this time, but only Thomas Smith of Layerthorpe, confronted the Chancellor. He managed to persuade Mr. Gladstone to lower the duty considerably.[5]

The chicory seed was usually imported from Belgium. Experiments in raising seed in Newark had been unsuccessful. The implements used for digging up the chicory, which were like parsnip roots, were similar to chisels or spade shafts. The tread on one side became sharp as a bayonet after years of use. Many implements were made at blacksmiths in Dunnington. In the 1850s there were twelve chicory drying kilns in that area.

However many of the Dunnington farmers were contracted out to Chicory Smith of Layerthorpe. The roots were washed in wooden troughs in the fields and were then transported to Layerthorpe and tipped in Chicory Yard, where they were sliced, dried and crushed until they ended up as grains as small as gunpowder. It was at this stage that they became subject to excise duty. They were then roasted in cylinders revolving over gas jets. It was said that after ten minutes on a foggy day, the fumes were so dense that the aroma clung to one's clothes.

By the turn of the century the industry began to die out. Considerable expense was involved in harvesting and cleaning the crop. The Belgians, who were the main exporters, had improved their appliances for drying the roots, and transport via the canals was much cheaper abroad. The kilns around Dunnington were left to decay around this time and the whole process was moved to York.[6]

The chicory works in Layerthorpe were in use until the early years of this century and some Dunnington farmers and labourers still remember their trips to Layerthorpe with their chicory roots. Thomas Smith who also had a works on the other side of the Foss near Lower Orchard Street, moved all his business there around this time. This building was demolished in 1967.[7]

Chapter IV. Notes and References

   (1) Y.R.L. *Y.E.P.* July 17 1913.

   (2) Information supplied by Mrs. M. Richardson, Field House, Heworth.

   (3) Reading, S. J. *The Derwent Valley Light Railway.* 3rd Ed. Oakwood press 1978.

   (4) Y.C.A. *Rate Books.* St. Cuthberts Parish 1850-1880.

   (5) Y.R.L. *Yorkshire Gazette.* 22-11-1902

   (6) Harris, A. *Chicory in Yorkshire.* Y.A.J. Vol. 59 1987.

   (7) Information supplied by Mr. Webster.

CHAPTER V

Shops in Edwardian Times

There were many small shops in Layerthorpe in the early part of this century. On the main street of a total of 105 properties, fifty of them were shops. Between numbers 1-40 there were thirty three shops. There were butchers and pork butchers, Ridsdell, Audin and Linfoot to name but a few. There were twelve general stores, Milners and Watsons, and J. H. Webster corn and flour dealer. On the main street, a milliner, poulterer and three greengrocers. There were also small shops down some of the side streets. In Redeness Street in 1902 there was Mrs. Wright, general stores; G. Wrigglesworth, confectioner; and G. Lockwood, grocer. In Bilton Street, Mrs. Paylor, general dealer; G. Wright, boot repairer; and H. Pygas, brush and toy dealer. Many people set up small shops in their front rooms and sold sweets and small items as no licence was needed to sell them. There was also a chemist, Fredrick Newey on the main street near the William IV public house. Mrs. Laycock and Mrs. Wrigglesworth were the local midwives and Messrs. Greenwood, Horwell, Laverack and Mellor, coal merchants.[1]

Although there wasn't a pawnshop in Layerthorpe much use was made of them. Mr. Webster remembered a woman who collected all the clothes and

Tom Horwell, coal merchant. Joss Horwell and Harry Mercer are on the cart. circa 1915.
Courtesy of the Horwell family

other articles in a pram to take to the pawnshop, Sharpes, at the corner of St. Savourgate each Monday morning. A suit or good coat would fetch eighteen shillings which would last the owners a week until pay-day when they would have to redeem their articles, paying one pound to get them back. The amount of money received for clothes depended on the condition of the garments . The amount received for each article decreased as the garment deteriorated.[2]

Branch No.8 of the York Equitable Industrial Society was opened in Layerthorpe in 1890. This was the forerunner of the York Co-operative Society, and was at the corner of Layerthorpe and St. Cuthbert's Road. In the 1930s it changed its name to the York Co-operative Society and had a grocery and butchering departments at No.76-80 Layerthorpe.[3]

Poverty and Parish Visiting Books

In the years 1900-1914 73% of the entire population of England lived in towns. The upper and middle classes represented only a quarter of the total of the population. 40% of the remaining population were engaged in manual work. The years 1900-1918 were exceptional in that real wages stopped rising, even falling slightly. This was partly due to a change in international trade which made imports more expensive. Real wages were stagnant in this period and prices rose due to the fact that British economy was responding less effectively to a changing trade situation. Britain's share in the world trade was steadily declining.

Charles Booth for London, and Seebohm Rowntree for York, in their surveys of people's wages and house keeping budgets, showed that over a quarter of the population lived below the poverty line. They could not afford the bare necessities such as food and warm clothing. For those people the price of food was very important indeed. The children suffered most, their growth was stunned, and mental powers cramped.[4]

Layerthorpe was considered one of the poorer areas of the city in the early part of the 20th century. At this time many of the inhabitants were skilled and semi-skilled men and labourers on low wages, unemployed men, widows and invalids who could not work. Many families were living in what Seebohm Rowntree had termed as secondary poverty. That is the family would just be able to manage if the wages were spent prudently. Many men spent much of their wages on drink and gambling and could not pay their debts.

The Reverend Fausset of St. Cuthbert's in his visits to his parishioners, found much evidence of marital dispute and even break up of families which he blamed on drink. In one family in Wilson's Yard, the husband was separated from his wife who had got him into trouble through drink and debts. In another family living in Hallfield Terrace, a woman with six children had moved in with another man and his children. Her husband had worked for the North Eastern Railway but was given to drink, and could not be found, so he did not support her. In Hallfield Road a mother was concerned for her son. He had been a good lad and received many Sunday School prizes but had now taken to drink like his father.[5]

Mr. Horwell, coal merchant, remembered fights in the streets especially after the pubs closed, women often as bad as men. Policemen would patrol the streets in twos and on one occasion a policeman had been thrown over Layerthorpe Bridge into the Foss. Mrs. Arnold remembered that many fights were caused by family feuds as much as drink. Families all living together in crowded and unsanitary conditions were often the reason. Many households consisted of individuals who could not work and had to rely on public assistance. One family living in Layerthorpe Buildings was very poor. The husband was a printer by trade but had been unemployed for a year. He now had a job in Selby but had to walk to work, a distance of nearly twelve miles. In another family in Kidd's Terrace, the husband only earned fifteen shillings a week chopping wood for the Corporation. One week he only earned eleven shillings and there were seven in that family. In Hallfield Road one lady was living on parish relief of only four shillings a week.[6]

Many wives had part time jobs to help the family income. Mrs. Collinson remembered her mother working as a knocker-up. She also had a paper round in Layerthorpe, for a Mr. Sharpe who had a shop at the corner of St. Savourgate. Mr. Webster's father was a joiner, living in Duke of York Street, he only earned eighteen shillings a week in 1902. There were eight in that family but fortunately his father had a small pension from the Boer War to help out. The problem seemed to be that the wages for a man in full time employment were not sufficient to support a large family, and large families were common place.[7]

Between 1905-14 the new Liberal governments, especially in the time of Lord Asquith, made considerable attempts to alleviate the problems of poverty. There were free school meals for the very poor children, and in 1909, old age pensions of five shillings a week were introduced. Before this, those who were unable to work, were sent to the Workhouse, unless they had families to care for them. Before 1910 there was no unemployment benefit, only parish relief. The receiving of this rendered the recipients paupers and as such they lost their right to citizenship. People would rather starve than go on parish relief.

The effects of the poverty on the children is shown in the Bilton Street school log books. The low attendance when the weather was bad was often due to the lack of shoes and suitable clothes. A report in the school log books for February 1900 reads:

"Bad weather, a snow storm, attendance very low"

October 1902 "A very wet day, attendance has fallen away owing to sickness and colds which are very prevalent owing chiefly to bad boots and scanty clothing especially of the younger boys".

Epidemics of measles, mumps and whooping cough closed the school for weeks. In 1904 and 1905 there was a scarlet fever epidemic, twenty boys being absent at one time. After the headmaster Mr. Jenkinson's daughter died in November 1904 the school was closed from November 1904 to January 1905. Poor nutrition and ill health also affected the ability of many children to learn at school. In January 1907 it was reported that "Several boys in Standard 1, who appear to be hopeless in spite of much work by teachers, and have made no progress, are a great drawback to the rest of the school".[8]

The church also organised concerts and outings and helped to combat poverty with charitable gifts. Canon Fausset's wife gave tea and sugar to families in Layerthorpe who were very poor, especially those with the husband out of work. There was a Sunday school along the front road belonging to St. Cuthbert's church which helped with the food and clothing.[9] Mrs. Lancaster lived next door to the Sunday School and was caretaker for many years. There was also a Wesleyan Mission Hall at the corner of Mansfield Street and Foss Islands Road. These premises were acquired in 1888 and sold in 1924. They became part of the York County Hygienic Laundry and when that closed were occupied by Craven's sweet firm until 1955.[10]

Layerthorpe Children 1929.

Early 20th. Century Inhabitants

From the parish visiting books of 1908/1909 we can glean a little about the lives of the people who lived in Layerthorpe in the early part of this century. The Rev. Fausset of St. Cuthbert's made a point of visiting all his parishioners, even if they were not Church of England and made little notes about some of the many families. Below is a selection of his jottings.

Layerthorpe Main Street

No.1 Mrs. Emma Brown has the public house, she lives with her granddaughter who is fifteen years old, and attends St. Michael Le Belfrey Sunday School.

Archway House

Mrs. J. Stephenson with six children who have no clothes for Sunday School. Her husband had been in hospital for ten weeks. He had an abscess taken from his lung. He talked about joining the Adult School when better. Had prayer with them.

No.21 Mr. & Mrs. J. H. Webster, corn merchant with one little girl. She goes to Priory Street School and St. Saviourgate Sunday School.

No.24 Mrs. Sissons lives here and has a bakers shop.

Portland Place

No.6 Mr. & Mrs. E. Jowett with six children. The wife goes to St. Lawrence's Church.

No.8 Mr. Henry Skelton with three children. They used to attend Sunday School but he could not agree with the teachers. Has the grocer's shop.

Layerthorpe Street

No. 5 Mr. & Mrs. John Stirk. Church people. Husband out of work.

No. 6 Mr. H. Trodd, publican, John Bull. One son and a niece who lives with them. Church people.

Layerthorpe Buildings

No.2 Mrs. Pratt with four children who attend the Catholic School. Many Protestant children attend the Catholic School.

Layerthorpe

No.15 Mrs. Walkington, widow, has the grocers shop. has lived in Layerthorpe all her life. Her husband died forty years ago and left her with seven children to bring up. Lives in the house over Archway.

Downhill Street

No.2   Mr. James Caulfield and six children who go to Layerthorpe Sunday School.

No.3   Mr. Willie Watson and wife. Children grown up. They have lived in Layerthorpe for twenty eight years, and seen the Rector and Curate once. Husband, a joiner has been out of work nearly two years.

No.13 Major Brown. He lost his leg in the war.

No.27 Mr. L. Wilde a Roman Catholic. Has the tobacconists shop.

No.33 Mr. & Mrs. Stranger with five children. They have no Sunday clothes to go to Sunday School. Husband out of work. My wife gave them tea and sugar. Some of the children have chicken pox.

Wilson's Terrace

No.17 Mrs. Watson with two children too young and delicate to attend Sunday School. Husband had to have an operation.

No.66 Mr. & Mrs. Laverack, coal merchant with three children. They attend Bilton Street School and Duke of York Sunday School.

Faber Street

No.35 Mr. Webster and wife, and six children who go to Hungate Mission. Had prayer with them.

Duke of York Street

Mr. Alderson and wife, and five children who go to Park Grove School and Duke of York   Sunday School. Children have measles.

Rymer Street

No.6   Mr. & Mrs. Marlow with four children, one has measles. They go to Bilton Street School. The husband attends the Adult School.

Hallfield Road

No.63 Mrs. Deighton, a widow for twenty six years. Her married daughter lives with her. She was on parish relief and had rheumatic gout. A very nice lady, had prayer with her.

Little Hallfield Road

No.4   Mrs. Bridges with two children, one has measles.

No.5   Mr. & Mrs. Bridges. Methodists. The woman very nice and a hard worker.

Kidd's Terrace

Mr. & Mrs. Dobson. Mrs. Dobson very poorly.

Bilton Street

No.1 Mr. Camidge and wife. Children too young to go to school.

No.2 Mr. J Addinall and wife and eight children.

No.3 Mr. & Mrs. Curran. Roman Catholics, wife very nice woman.

No.6 Mrs. May Field, a widow, has bronchitis.

No.8 Mr. George Labon and wife, both invalids.

No.8 Martha Watson, a widow with one son who works at Rowntrees, one son in hospital and a lodger who is out of work.

No.11 Mr. & Mrs. G Varley, six children who go to Salem Sunday School.

No.12 Mrs. Deighton, very deaf.

No.38 Mr. & Mrs. T Horwell with seven children who go to Duke of York Mission Hall. Wife goes to St. Cuthbert's.

No.43 Mr. & Mrs. Wright with five children, they have a shoe maker's shop.

No.46 Mr. & Mrs. W Webb have the public house. The Grandma and Grandad live with them.

No.47 Mr. Frankish with five children. The wife is in hospital

No.65 Mr. & Mrs. G Lockwood who have a grocer's shop.

Redeness Street

No.2 Mrs. Richardson, a widow, she used to be the church sexton but has bad eyes now.

No.4 Mr. George Patrick has the public house. Three children.

No.6 Jessie Burley. She was the caretaker of the Adult school

No.15 Mr. & Mrs. James Seale with five children.

No.16 Mr. & Mrs. Woodcock with seven children.

No.23 Mr. & Mrs. Greenwood, the father is out of work. They have seven children.[11]

Faber Street Peace Treat. 1919.

Young Ladies from Faber Street Area. 1919.

Courtesy of D. Poole

Residents from Kidd's Terrace. 1919.

Children from Kidd's Terrace. 1919.

Courtesy of D. Poole

*Primitive Methodists

William Clowes, the Primitive Methodist Evangelist, first preached in York in May 1819. Sarah Kirkland and Sarah Harrison, well known Evangelists, also preached later that same summer. As a result of these early visits and meetings, with encouragement of "friends" from Elvington, a small society of seven members was formed in 1820 and met in a chapel in Grape Lane. The York branch expanded, and moved from Grape Lane to the Ebenezer Chapel in Little Stonegate, which became the basis for all the later groups and chapels built in other areas of York. In the summer of 1874, the Primitive Methodists held open air meetings in Layerthorpe. In the winter they rented two rooms in Lawson's Yard, off Bilton Street, where meetings and services were held for three years. In 1877 a chapel was built in a large yard at the back of two houses in Duke of York Street, costing £700. A passage through one house became the entrance to the chapel, which was known as the Duke of York Mission Rooms. It had a seating capacity for 190 people, a small organ and good heating and ventilation and became part of York's first Primitive Methodist Circuit, Monkgate Circuit.[12] It had a good Sunday School and many Layerthorpe children attended. It played an important part in fighting against poverty in Victorian and Edwardian times. It was still in use in 1955. Mrs. M Richardson was the caretaker for many years.[13]

Layerthorpe Adult School

The early foundations of the Adult School movement in York, were laid down by a few families of Quaker tradesmen and the young men in their employment. Adult schools originated in Nottingham in 1798. William Singleton a Methodist opened a school for the purpose of teaching reading and writing, and was later joined by Samuel Fox a Quaker who was a grocer. The school met at seven on a Sunday morning. Men and Women were admitted but met in separate rooms. In 1816 similar schools were established by friends in Leeds and York, one teacher being Samuel Tuke.

The Adult School movement as we know it today may be regarded as having started its career with the establishment of a school in Birmingham by Joseph Sturge which spread to York in 1856. The York Adult School movement had its origin in Hope Street just inside Walmgate Bar.

In December 1904 the Layerthorpe Adult School opened in Redeness Street. The school stared as a result of a speech given in York in 1903 by William Crook, the champion of Adult schools. Several local men met and decided to start a school in Layerthorpe. Frank Rowntree came from the Hope Street School, to stand as president. G Mansfield and S Adams of Heworth Croft, were vice presidents. G & J Ridsdel, C Leng, A Newlove,

W Harrison and J Haw, were on the first committee. The meetings were first held in the Duke of York chapel, but in 1902 two houses in Redeness Street were demolished for the building of a school and social club. There was a large hall for meetings and a library and two bathrooms on the first floor. There were facilities above for playing darts, billiards and dominoes.(14) As well as teaching people to read and write the school provided a social club where concerts and outings were organised. Many societies which were formed at this time had their headquarters in the Adult School. There were cycling, angling and cricket clubs. Mr. Butcher the MP for York opened the building. He remarked on the fact that this club was the one place where the conservative lamb could lie down with the radical lion, it was non political. He went on to say that to take to drink was the worst kind of recreation and to indulge in gambling, a bad thing. Those who associated with the adult school found better and higher amusements.(15)

The Public Houses

Many of the Layerthorpe inhabitants were attracted to the life in the local public houses. There they could find warmth and friendliness. In the early part of this century there were six in this area and they opened from early morning until very late at night. Mr. Webster remembered hearing singing in the pubs as he went to school. Some men went in before work and never got to work. Layerthorpe Bridge Inn was situated in a building on the Layerthorpe Bridge. It later became Walker's offices, but the buildings are now demolished. The Bridge Inn was a very lively pub, and in the 1890s was a venue for linnet singing competitions.(16)

Only a few doors away stood the John Bull pub. This was first mentioned as a public house in the street directories of the 1830s. In 1903 it was a free house and brewed its own beer at a 1d a pint. It was owned then by a Mr. Nicholson of Acomb and the landlord was a Mr. H R Trodd. At that time there was a great number of public houses in York and there was a move then to close some of them. The John Bull was one such pub along with the Blue Bell of Fossgate and the Red Lion of Merchantgate. However it was spared then as it was said it had been licensed for 70 years with never a conviction against it or its landlord.(17)

The original building comprised a group of cottages, a shop and the pub. There was a passage running through the centre of the complex giving access to several small cottages in the yard, John Bull Yard. It was bought by John Smith Brewery Company of Tadcaster in 1915. The original buildings were altered in 1937 and a new front in the Brewers Tudor style was added. The pub was run as a tied house until 1979 when it was closed. It was bought by motor trader, Mr. Turnbull who applied for permission to change its use to a shop with flats. He used it as a store for his garage until 1982 when Mr. Neville Hobson took on a lease and started it as a pub again. When the lease ran out, Mr. Turnbull wished to knock it down and use the land as an extension to his showroom. After a long campaign to keep it open, the John Bull was finally closed in May 1994. The 1930s furniture and fittings and tin backed advertisements were sold off at auction. The pub was demolished in 1995.[18]

The King William IV public house was between the John Bull and the Frog Hall, and known as the middle pub. This was closed in the 1930s and became flats. The Bridge Inn and the Kings Arms in Bilton Street were closed in 1921. The Frog Hall was mentioned in the 18th. century leases in the York City House books, called then Frog Hall Tavern. It was altered in the 1930s. There was another public house in Redeness Street called The George IV. run by the Patrick family for many years, but was only licensed to sell beer, and known as a beer house. Many early societies held their first meetings in the public houses. They also organised many outings and excursions. The Frog Hall is the only pub left in Layerthorpe now.[19]

Layerthorpe Working Men's Club

The first meetings of Layerthorpe men to discuss opening a Working Men's Club were held in the Frog Hall and Shoulder of Mutton public house on Heworth Green. Layerthorpe Working Men's club was eventually opened in October 1908 in a house at the corner of Duke of York Street. Many of the first members then had to sit on crates to drink their pints until local plumber Mr. Hall donated the first chair. Gradually the premises increased from one house to six houses. In addition to the main room, there was a ladies room downstairs, while on the first floor there were bathrooms and committee rooms, and a large billiards room with two tables. The founder members were, Billy Watson, Bert Jackson, Walter Scarth, Joe Alderson, Harry Kilby and R. Preston. Others who helped the club to become established were, Mr. W. Early, the first president, T. E. Watson, Harry Archer, P. Welsh, Alf Bolton, H. Clark, A. Adams, F. Pullin, J. Simpson, F. Gill and E. Allison. The club claimed to have been the first of the York clubs to organise children's outings. Walking, fishing, rugby and bowls matches were organised every year.[20] In the 1960s when the houses in Duke of York Street were demolished, a new working men's club was built in Little Hallfield Road, which is still there to day.

Layerthorpe Bowling Club was formed in 1933, many of the first members had originally bowled for Heworth, but wished to start their own club. C. Barnett, C. Doughty, F. Foster, F. G. Hemenway, C. Horner, A. Mercer and A Shephard were some of the first members. This became a very successful bowling club, and in 1941 won all the local championships. This club is still flourishing today.[21]

Layerthorpe Bowling Club 1941
Back Row: J. Donley, J. Good, G. North, F. Foster, B. W. Poole, E. Holmes, Mr. Jefferson, G. Watson, F. Brewer, H. Mayfield.
Middle Row: Rev. Bainton, C. Leng, A. Anderson, W. Curtis, A. Crumbie, W. Gillis, A. Allen, R. Calam, J. Bolton, F. G. Hemingway, E. Fletcher.
Front Row: T. Stirk, J. Ward, C. Barnett, t. Calvert, H. Horner, Master Bolton

Courtesy of D. Poole

Chapter V. Notes and References

(1) Kelly's *York Directory,* 1902.

(2) Information supplied by Mr. Webster.

(3) Kelly's 1890, 1930.

(4) Rowntree, B. S. Poverty. *A Study of Town Life.* 3rd ed. London 1908.

(5) Borthwick. *St. Cuthbert's Parish visiting books.* (1907-1909). 48-54.

(6) Ibid.

(7) Information supplied by Mrs. Collinson, Mr. Webster.

(8) Y.C.A. *Bilton Street Log Books.* 1900, 1904, 1905, 1907.

(9) Borthwick. PRY/CU. 1909. 48-54

(10) Y.R.L. Kellys. 1888-1924, 1955

(11) Borthwick. PRY/CU. (1908-1909). 48-54.

(12) Camidge, W. *Methodism in York.* (Weslyan Methodist Conference York 1908)

(13) Information supplied by Mrs. Richardson.

(14) Gilman, F. J. *Story of York Adult Schools.* Delittle & Fenwick.1907.31.

(15) Y.RL. York Gazette and Herald. 14 December 1904.

(16) Information supplied by Mr. Webster. Mr. D Poole, Penygent Avenue York.

(17) Peacock, A. J. *York 1900-1914.* York Settlement Trust. 64

(18) Y.R.L.. Y.E.P. 30 March 1994.

(19) Information supplied by Mr. D. Poole.

(20) Y.R.L. *History of York Working Men's Clubs.* Y. 331.83.

(21) Information supplied by Mr. F. Hemenway, Wood St. York.

CHAPTER VI

For King and Country

The Great War or First World War began on August 4th 1914. In that same month the Royal Flying Corps arrived on the Knavesmire where an aerodrome had been constructed. The Knavesmire was the site of the Blackburn Aeroplane Company. At first, the reservists were called up and on August 16th the troops departed by train and guns appeared on Bootham Stray. There was a great shortage of horses and many had to be commandeered from the farms.[1]

In 1916, conscription was introduced for the first time in British history. War fever was very high and photographs of families serving in the war appeared in the papers. The Bilton Street School log books contain many references to old boys serving abroad. Many came back on leave to visit their old school.

1915 Feb. 2nd	"Private Varley and Laverack came to visit the school today. Private Laverack is recovering from frost bite but will shortly be returning to the front".
February 16th.	"The school was visited by Henry Ward an old scholar who is now in the navy. His experiences in the North Sea engagements, and his description of a sailor's life during war time were very interesting".
July 1st.	"Ten pairs of socks, knitted by the girls department have been sent to the old boys serving at the front, with twelve boxes of cigarettes".
November 29th.	"Visit by J. Binks from the trenches in France near Ypres, brought fur coat and respirator to show children".
December 10th.	"Fifty pairs of mittens sent to the front".
1916 July 20th.	"Visit by Lieutenant W. Robinson, an old scholar risen from the ranks to an officer".
September 27th.	"Attendance low today, many boys unwell due to air raid, this part of the city being especially affected".

The affects of the war on the children were also shown in the log books. With fathers away from home and mothers engaged in munitions work, many children had to stop at home to look after younger children and also do the shopping.

In December 1916 it was reported. "No margarine or butter to be had in Layerthorpe, and boys absent because they had gone into the town to hunt for supplies".[2]

In 1916, zeppelins flew over and bombed York on three occasions, causing considerable damage to the Heworth and Nunnery lane areas. War fever was high, and the papers contained many accounts of the families serving abroad. There was a report of the Wheatley family of Layerthorpe with nine relatives serving in the war, and the exploits of one Gunner Townsend of Downhill Street make fascinating reading. He was the son of Mr. J. H. Townsend and one of a family of fighting brothers. He went out with the expeditionary force to France and Belgium, was wounded on the Somme in October 1916 and sent to a Scottish hospital to recuperate. After convalescing in York, he was again ordered overseas. Whilst on route to the port of embarkation, the train in which he was travelling broke in two, the portion in which he was a passenger was left behind. He finally managed to board the troop ship Cameronia which was torpedoed on April 5th 1917 in the Mediterranean. He drifted in a raft for three days before being picked up and spent eleven days in Alexandria recovering from exhaustion. After leaving that port the vessel he was travelling in was wrecked, again and he spent several days on an island in true Robinson Crusoe fashion before being rescued and granted special leave to return home to Layerthorpe. One of his brothers, Private J. Townsend of the Scots Guards was killed in action, Private Edward was disabled. Private Frederick of the Northumberland Fusiliers was invalided out from the front, whilst his brother Alfred was still abroad with the Scottish Rifles.[3]

Corporal John Howden with his mobile Xray unit. Salonika, 1917.
Courtesy of the Borthwick Institute

In November 1917, the Rev. Pyne of St. Cuthbert's, received a letter from Corporal John Howden of the Mobile Xray Unit, stationed in Salonika, home address was Downhill Street, Layerthorpe. He was asking if it would be possible for a gramophone and records to be sent out to help ease the loneliness of the evenings there. The Rev. Pyne put a notice in the Yorkshire Herald, but according to another letter was unsuccessful in his attempts to send them out a gramophone.[4]

In January 1918 several old boys visited the school wearing military medals, among them being Sergeant Deighton, Quarter Master Utterly and Private Garbutt. At one time three hundred old boys were serving in the war. The pay was one shilling a day and tuppence extra per day if there were children.

The Great War ended on November 11th. 1918 but peace celebrations were not held until the following summer. Street parties were held in every part of the city, and on August 20th. six thousand scholars attended a thanksgiving service in York Minster. The children had special treats in the schools, and each child was presented with a banana and a quarter of a pound of chocolates.[5]

Schools

In the November of 1919, Mr. Jenkinson, headmaster of Bilton Street School for many years, resigned because of ill health, and Mr. F.W. Scaife was appointed to that post. He improved the standard of education in the school with his system of "houses" and greater co-operation between pupils and teachers. John Welch was the first pupil from the school to gain "The Lady Hewley's Scholarship" to Nunthorpe Grammar School.[6]

In the early years of this century there was a great deal of overcrowding in the school. In 1912, the infants department was moved to premises in St. Cuthbert's Road, which became known as Layerthorpe Infant's School. This building had been given as a gift in 1909 to the York Education Committee, by Mr. C. Mills of 33 Bootham, a city magistrate. It had been built for him in 1905 to use as a school or club for the working class lads of that area.

In the 1920's, the large house "Layerthorpe Grove" and garden which still stands on the corner of Mill Lane and Hawthorn Terrace, known then as Layerthorpe Road, was purchased by the Education Committee. This house had been previously owned by the Millington family. It was bought by Mr. Arnold Rowntree after the death of Miss Elizabeth Millington in 1918 and sold to York Corporation in 1920. Infants from St. Cuthbert's Road School were transferred there, and it was used as a school until 1928, when the new Tang Hall Schools were opened. It was bought by Mr. Albert London in the

Children at the Layerthorpe Infant's School, circa 1920.   *Courtesy of Mrs. M. White*

1930's called then Millington House, and from that sale developed what is now known as London's Newsagents and Toy Shop.[7]

In April 1921, it was reported in the school log books, that several boys were absent from school searching York for coal because of the miner's strike. There was also a great shortage of coal in the school, and often on very cold days they were unable to have fires .

The school baths, which had been in use since 1910, were closed in 1928. Mrs. Arnold remembered them when she was a child and the luxury of having a bath. She said that everyone was asked if they would like one, and no one thought it was beneath their dignity to accept. When there wasn't a bathroom at home it was lovely to get into a hot bath. The caretaker's wife did the bathing.

In 1928, Mr. Scaife left Bilton Street School to become headmaster of the newly opened "Avenue" School, part of the new Tang Hall School complex. Bilton Street was reorganised as an Infant School in 1930, and the Juniors went to Heworth or Tang Hall Schools.

In June 1932 the school celebrated its Centenary. The children were given a tea party at the school and presented with a mug. The children, dressed in Victorian clothes entertained their parents in the evening with a concert of songs and dancing. A large birthday cake was cut by Mrs. Jane Brammall, who had been a pupil in 1863.[8]

St. Cuthbert's Church

In 1595, St. Mary's Church Layerthorpe, was demolished and the parish was joined to St. Cuthbert's. This church was originally erected about, 687 AD., in a place said to have been blessed by St.Cuthbert himself. The existing building dates from 1430, when it was restored and rebuilt by William de Bowes, Lord Mayor of York.

St. Cuthbert's is one of York's oldest churches, and over a period of nearly 400 years the Layerthorpe community was served by its many rectors. Below is a summary of the work of just three of them from Victorian times to the present day.

We begin with the Reverend Canon Fausset, rector for fifty years, from 1859 until his death in 1910. It was he who saw the parish grow as more and more houses were built and the community evolved. Parish records show how active he was in establishing charities and trusts, which proved so vital for people living in this poor and over populated area. In 1892, he arranged for three patient's tickets for the York Dispensary to be given annually for the benefit of his parishioners. In 1905, he donated one hundred pounds to the funds of the County Hospital to ensure that three in patient and six out patient recommendations were issued annually to himself and succeeding Rectors of St. Cuthbert's.

A coal charity and an educational trust were among other facilities which he set up to help his parishioners. It was Canon Fausset's practice to visit every household in the parish at regular intervals and his visiting books show that he held no bias towards those of his own faith, but discussed problems and prayed with anyone in need.[9]

Canon Fausset was succeeded by the Rev. Reginald Gaynesford Pyne, appointed by the Archbishop of York on March 26th. 1910, and inducted by the Bishop of Beverley on 11 July in the same year. He was destined to serve for twenty four years until February 1934. He is remembered today with affection and respect by those Layerthorpe people who knew him.

His vestry minutes paint a detailed picture of life in Layerthorpe, and take the form of a review of events in the previous year. Mr. Pyne's enthusiasm and love of the community shine through in these records. In 1910, Mr. Pyne decided to endeavour to restore the church and increase its endowment as a memorial to the late Canon Fausset. The need for restoration must have been very apparent, because in February 1911 the church was closed as the roof was unsafe. The Sunday School room was then licensed for divine service. Progress with restoration work was reported the following year, when Mr. Pyne also recommended consideration be given to the appointment of female church wardens (women having the parliamentary vote by that time).

The church was reopened on December 3rd 1912 by Archbishop Cosmo Gordon Lang. Electric lighting was installed and said to be the first in any church in the country. Four hundred and fifty pounds was still needed to complete the restoration.

In his review of 1913, Mr. Pyne reported one hundred and eighty pounds still required to meet expenditure on the restoration. He had, by then, revived the custom of "beating the parish bounds" formerly used to ascertain exact boundaries for rating purposes. Good work was also being done with the revival of St. Cuthbert's Junior's Annual Race and the starting of the parish magazine. This had a circulation of four hundred per month and one thousand parish almanacs were distributed to each house in the parish.

1914 saw the start of the First World War and records over the next four years concentrate greatly on its effects on the parish. By April 1915, almost three hundred parishioners were on active service and the following year this had risen to five hundred and fifty (a number larger in proportion than any other parish in York). Sympathy was shown to all bereaved families and a memorial service held in the church in each case.[10]

During an air raid on May 2nd 1916, a Zeppelin bomb in St. Saviour's Place killed several people in a lodging house. Two parishioners, who were passing by at the time also lost their lives, Sgt. Edward Gordon Beckett who was on leave, and Mr. Benjamin Sharpe.

Throughout the war years steady work continued in the parish. The girls' day school won the York Rounders Championship in 1915, 1916 and 1917 and the Boys' Club played a useful role despite many helpers being on active service. The Rev. Pyne was president of the York and District Band of Hope and in 1916 St. Cuthbert's provided the May Queen, Florence Peacock.

Soon after the war ended, Mr. Pyne presided over a special meeting of parishioners to consider a suitable memorial for the men of the parish who had fallen in the war. Over one hundred and twenty had lost their lives and "It seemed fitting that as their graves were so far away, some record be made to preserve their remembrance". It was resolved that a tablet be placed in the church and the names of all who served (more than eight hundred and fifty) should be inscribed in an album. A subsequent meeting agreed to endeavour to raise one hundred pounds, and to this end a house to house collection and other fund-raising events were organised. Whist drives, rugby matches and social evenings brought entertainment and recreation to the area at the same time as money was raised to honour friends and relatives.

July and August 1919 saw a celebration of peace, marked by informal street parties throughout the parish. The War Memorial was unveiled on January 22nd 1921 and is in two parts. Inside the church an oak tablet inscribed with the names and dates of all those who lost their lives, bears the dedication "Sacred to the memory of the men from this parish who gave their lives for King and Country in the Great War 1914-1918". Outside, by the door is a memorial cross "to be an open air memorial of divine strength and human courage in conflict".

In the years following the war, Mr. Pyne was deeply involved with youth work in the parish. He reported with pride the achievement of both the boys' and girls' schools in winning trophies for swimming, football and gymnastics. He also gave support and encouragement to the Boys' Club. Former Layerthorpe residents, who were children then, remember the excitement which filled the air whenever Mr. Pyne appeared in their street on his bicycle. All would clamour to him, waiting to be lifted up and given rides. He always had time and a word for them. Small wonder then, that in

Rev. Reginald Gaynesford Pyne. *Courtesy of Mrs. M. White*

1924 he was able to refer to the "spirit of unity and good will which pervades the parish" and to say in 1930 that "the church is in constant use for baptisms, marriages and funerals".

St. Cuthbert's Church was the scene of the first service by wireless in York. This took place on February 14th 1925 after the 6.30 service and was probably one of the first ever in a church in England.

Two boys, Fred Richardson and Ernest Kingham, both aged 16 sailed for Canada on March 28th 1924 under the Salvation Army Boys Migration Scheme in which Mr. Pyne was involved. Raymond Smith, Arthur and Albert Kynman followed a year later. In 1932, Mr. Pyne was involved with the arrangements for home visit tickets, to enable boys who had "gone out from Great Britain to the Empire to visit their former homes".[11]

Press reports of Mr. Pyne's sudden and untimely death in February 1934 conveyed the sadness and sense of loss experienced in the parish. Seldom have so many people turned out to witness a funeral procession; police were on duty to deal with the crowds. The Yorkshire Herald reported "He was heart and soul in his parochial work in connection with which he laboured tirelessly. Blinds in every house were lowered as the cortege passed through Layerthorpe, house wives came to the doors , many of them weeping. Each side of Layerthorpe was lined with people and the church was filled with people from the parish. For two hours afterwards, people filed past the coffin resting in the main aisle at the foot of the sanctuary steps". At a memorial service on February 18th when the Rural Dean preached, it is reported the church was full and people were sitting on the floor[12]

The next incumbent, The Rev. Reginald Bainton took up his duties on July 1st 1934, coming from his previous post as Vicar of Hawsker, to a parish whose population was declining, due to the demolition of a large number of houses leading to the River Foss.

At his first Parish Council meeting held shortly after his arrival, Mr. Bainton discussed a memorial to Mr. Pyne, and also suggested setting up mixed bible classes for young people over the age of fourteen. By the end of the year, more than one hundred pounds was deposited in the Memorial Fund and it was decided this should be used to provide a stained glass window at the west end of the church, dedicated to St. Cuthbert. A design was accepted in February 1935, and the window was unveiled at a service attended by the Archbishop of York on November 2nd.

Social activities continued, but matters of finance were of great concern with funds needed for repairs to the church and for the choir. The following year saw declining attendances and collections as people moved to other parishes following more slum clearance, with a further forty houses soon to be demolished.

Demolition of houses continued until the outbreak of War in 1939 and receipts and church attendance continued to decline. Additional problems arose during the War with the need to protect and darken windows and to insure against War damage. Nethertheless the community spirit remained and a small number of social events were held each year as the parish adapted to the circumstances of War.

Following the War, church life became more stable, but the social changes occurring in all walks of life led to a decline in attendance and a lowering of the importance of the church in people's lives. By 1953 finance was fairly satisfactory but , "attendance at Holy Communion was very small and caused new and young communicants discouragement".

In December 1960, tenders were invited for the demolition of one hundred and forty five houses in the Layerthorpe area, with more to follow in two years. Mr. Bainton saw his once thriving church and congregation diminish to a trickle with only a small handful of regular worshipers.[13]

In July 1965, the Rev. David Watson and his wife Ann arrived at St. Cuthbert's, a church due to be made redundant in 1966 and serving an area which looked much like a bomb site. Mr. Watson was a young man with vision, enthusiasm and tremendous skills as a preacher and with people. His success brought him world wide fame before his premature death in 1984.

His preaching skills at St. Cuthbert's soon became known, and in December 1965 he held his first family service. The Parish was united with Holy Trinity Heworth in 1966 and an increasing congregation was drawn from a wider area. There soon followed a Christian Nightschool, Youth Fellowship and the introduction of sketches and drama into services.

By 1973, congregations were so large and the church so overcrowded that evening services were moved to the larger church of St. Michael le Belfrey which was under utilised. David Watson was then appointed Vicar of St. Michael's and ultimately all services were transferred to that church.

St. Cuthbert's has become the Administration Centre for St. Michael le Belfrey and the interior of the church has been sympathetically altered to meet the needs of its new function. Happily, the War Memorial and the Pyne Memorial Window remain, along with other important features as a reminder of former times. Whilst the building is primarily an administrative centre, as a consecrated building, it remains available for official services, such as marriages. A Ministry to the Poor continues through its use as one of the bases for the City's soup kitchen. Staff at the recently opened M.A.F.F. building hold regular prayer meetings in the church thus continuing in small part its role in the parish as a place of worship.[14]

Chapter VI. Notes and References

(1) Y.R.L. *Yorkshire Gazette* August 1914.

(2) Y.C.A. *Bilton Street Logbooks* 1915, 1916.

(3) Y.R.L. *Yorkshire Herald* July. December 1917.

(4) Borthwick PR/CU 76 A.

(5) Y.C.A. *Logbooks* 1918.

(6) Ibid. 1919, 1920.

(7) Y.C.A. *Council Minutes,* 1909, 1920.

(8) Y.C.A. *Logbooks* 1921, 1928, 1932.

(9) St. Cuthbert's Church. *A Short History*

(10) Borthwick. *Vestry Minutes*. PRY/CU 32-36.

(11) Ibid.

(12) Y.R.L. *Yorkshire Herald,* 15th February 1934.

(13) Borthwick. PRY/CU 32-36.

(14) St. Cuthbert's Church, *Papers of the Administrative Centre for St. Michael le Belfrey.*

Mr. Fred Waite outside his shop in Layerthorpe, 1930. *Courtesy of Mrs. S. Davies*

CHAPTER VII

Shops and Industries 1920s and 1930s

What was it like to live in Layerthorpe in the 1920s & 30s?

On Foss bank there would have been J. H. Walker, builder's coal yard. This firm had been established in 1907. Mr. Walker was originally a farmer from Easingwold. He started his business in Fulford then moved to Layerthorpe in 1907. Mr. S. H. Smith was the works manager then, but became an equal partner in the firm after the war. They brought coal and sand to their builder's yard in their own barge, "Reklaw", Walker spelt backwards.

Mr. Mercer had the newsagent's shop next to the John Bull , taking over from Mr. Waite, when he moved to be landlord of the pub next door.[1] Stirk's furnishing stores expanded in the 1930s and took up the space formerly occupied by six houses, No. 21-27. Many young couples set up their first home with furniture from Stirk's. They sold good quality furniture at a reasonable price. The Stirk family first appeared in the records for Layerthorpe in the early 1900s.

There were many grocers and greengrocers at this time, Booths, Holmes, and Milners on the main Layerthorpe road, and Pratts, Currans, Metcalfes, Clarks, Hugills, Burns, Watsons and Keys listed as general dealers. Botterills and Holmes, fruiterers and florists.[2] Mrs. Finch remembered her grandmother, Mrs. Milner who had a general store in Layerthorpe in the 1920s and 30s , She sold green vegetables, fruit, milk and all kinds of varied merchandise. Some people paid cash on the spot, others paid later.[3]

Mrs. Poole remembered her parent's shop near the corner of Duke of York Street, " Billy Watsons". She said her mother's shop opened from 7am to 10pm originally, but later on when new laws were brought in they had to close at 8pm. However, people came and knocked at the side door after closing time. People paid cash, but when they fell on hard times they could pay on "tick", which was all recorded in a book. She said there was a lot of poor people in Layerthorpe in the 20s & 30s and a lot of unemployment then, but most people paid back their debts when they could.[4]

There were many bakers and confectioners at this time. Hardcastles and Nicholsons were just two. People remembered queuing for home made bread at Hardcastles, and Mrs. Nicholson was renowned for her mouth watering meat pies.[5] There were several newsagents and tobacconists, Mercers, Acklams, Skinners and Skerry. Hairdressers, Greenwoods and Wilsons. Their were plenty of clothes shops and dressmakers. Miss Skinner near the Frog Hall and the two shops owned by the "Miss" Smiths in Hart's

Terrace, one shop selling ladies clothes, the other children's outfits. Their was also Thompsons, later Masons, and Clarks selling cycles and wirelesses. In Hart's Terrace, Mr. Harrison had his car and taxi business. Most of the side streets had their corner shops and off licences, such as Grays at the corner of Rymer Street, later to become Liddles, Long's off licence in Richmond Street and Thompsons off licence in Hallfield Road. In the 1930s there was also a fried fish shop and wet fish dealer in Hallfield Road.[6]

Life in the 1920s and 1930s

Mrs. Elsie Johnson, Mrs. Olive King and Mrs. Minnie White, were sisters, and as girls lived in Redeness Street in the 1920s. Their mother, Mrs. Gibson died when her youngest child was only three. There were twelve in the family. Mr. W Gibson, their father, with the help of their sister Annie, aged fourteen, brought them all up. The girls remembered some of the shopkeepers and characters who lived in Layerthorpe in their youth. They recalled the feel in their hands of corn stocked by J. H. Webster corn merchant. They remembered the lovely tea cakes from Brier Hardcastle's cake shop, and how he always wrapped everything up in yellow tissue paper. He stocked boxes of Peek Frean biscuits. They recalled the chemist, Mr. Newey, with his shop on the main road near Layerthorpe Buildings. He wore a black pill box hat and they thought as children, that the sign W. Newey, M.P.S. meant:- "Mr. Newey makes people sick". They remembered seeing the mice running out of potato sacks in the green grocers, and visiting Mr. Blanchard the cobbler who always seemed to have his mouth full of shoe tacks.

They would often run errands for old ladies in their street. One lady would send them to the George IV public house for her daily jug of beer but always put the red hot poker in it before drinking. Another old lady always wore a flat cap and "harden" apron and would always cook her meals the night before. They would rarely receive money for the jobs they did but would often receive just a few sweets or a biscuit. They remembered the cattle going down Layerthorpe to the slaughter house in Wilson's Yard. Once a sheep escaped and became stuck down their house passage. They all hid in the pantry until the sheep was caught, but had to clean up all the sheep's droppings afterwards. Boys would take the bladders of slain animals from the slaughter house, blow them up and tie them on sticks to hit and chase the girls with.

Mrs. O. King helped the school caretaker, Mr. Allinson, to clean out the school fires. She was often allowed to take home the cinders. She also remembered the baths at the school, and being scrubbed by the caretaker with carbolic soap. She also did handicraft work, leather work and country dancing at the Adult School in Redeness Street. When she was a teenager she attended "penny dances" at St. Cuthbert's Road School.[7]

Mrs. Hale remembered, how her great grandfather, Mr. John Watkinson had lived for many years in Redeness Street in the 1920s. He was very skilled in carving wood and stone, his house contained many examples of his work. He lived there until he died in his nineties.[8]

Mrs. Wakelin's husband's family had a shop in Layerthorpe, and she recalled that there was a lot of poverty in the 1920s in that area. Lads would go barefoot as shoes were one shilling a pair. She remembered the herring man with his barrow full of fresh herrings at 3d and 6d each (enough to feed a family) and milk at halfpenny a pint. Coal was one shilling and four pence for ten stone.[9]

Mr. Cole remembered his father, Mr. Fred Cole, who worked at the Co-operative Stores in Layerthorpe in its early years. He lived for many years in Rymer Street and was a keen angler, winning the All England championship in 1912 at Skip Bridge, near Nun Monkton.[10]

All the children used to enjoy the buskers who frequented the streets. They remembered "Burlington Bertie" with his song and dance routine, the man with the organ and monkey and the man with the accordion. Boxing day was the time when all the children used to queue up outside the shops for their Christmas boxes, usually an apple or orange or if lucky a new penny.

In the summer months, the children would play hop scotch and rounders in the streets or play on the swings in the recreation ground at the bottom of St. Cuthbert's Road. They would often watch their dads and older brothers play illegal games such as "pitch and toss" in the yards, keeping a watch out for the police. Sometimes older children would mischievously rush up shouting "police!" to try and find any money left behind in the panic. Illegal gambling also took place at some corner shops and "Bookies Runners" and "Look Out" men were all part of the life at this time.

York County Hygienic Laundry

This laundry was opened around 1904 in Foss Islands Road. The Boss, Mr. H.E. Clark, lived at "The cottage" at the corner of Foss Islands Road and Layerthorpe. This laundry not only took in laundry from private houses and private schools in York, but also from hotels as far away as Scarborough. During the war years it did the laundry of many service men.

Many Layerthorpe women and girls were employed at the laundry. Mrs. King remembered starting work there aged fourteen years in 1929. She said the work was very hard, and in the summer the heat was unbearable. Unions were not encouraged, and even when she became a supervisor she

Staff of the York County Hygiene Laundry, circa 1940. *Courtesy of Mrs. B. Hugill*

said her wage was not as much as her sister received at Rowntree's factory. She recalled the sheets going through the big rollers, two women feeding the sheets and two folding them as they came out. Her aunt worked there until she was seventy, along with other women she just scrubbed clothes all day. She remembered on hot days seeing their faces pouring with sweat.

Clothes were ironed with big gas irons, special irons being used for cuffs and collars. Blankets were hung up to air and dry in large airing rooms. Carpets were cleaned in a room in Mansfield Street which had formerly been the Weslyan Mission Rooms.[11]

York Gas Company

York Gas Light Company was established in 1823 and works were built on land on the banks of the River Foss near Monk Bridge. On the evening of the 23rd March 1824 gas was supplied to all major streets and shops in the City and the Minster bells were rung to usher in a new era of light. In 1837, a rival gas company, York Union Gas Light Company was formed and works were built near the Foss in Hungate. After seven years of dispute the two companies amalgamated in 1844 to form the York Gas Company. The new enlarged works had its own railway system with overhead sidings and a bridge over the Foss. This rail line linked up with the Foss Islands branch of the North Eastern Railway which enabled coal to be transported straight to the works.

Although the gas works were not strictly in Layerthorpe, the houses in Wilson's Row, Wilson's Yard, Vicar's Terrace and Vicar's Row backed onto the gas holders. Some of these properties were tied houses for employees of the gas works. The large white gasometer which was of German manufacture was erected in the 1920s. During the War years it was painted in camouflage colours and used for fire watching.

Many Layerthorpe men were employed at the gas works. Fawdington Lane still runs from Layerthorpe through the gas work's land to Heworth Green.[12]

Taylor's Engineering Works

This family business was started in the early 1900s by Charles James Taylor who had previously worked as a foreman at the railway. It began in a cobbler's shop in a yard just off the main Layerthorpe road near St.Cuthbert's Sunday School. Mr. Taylor was a whitesmith by trade and his son Albert followed in his footsteps becoming managing director of the firm when his father died in 1929. In the 1930s the business expanded and properties in Chicory Yard and Portland Place were bought, creating workshops on both sides of the road. During the War years they made iron beds for soldiers and parts for tractors and bailey bridges. There are evidences of their craftsmanship around York today . At the height of their prosperity they employed forty workmen and four to five office staff. Many York lads served their apprenticeships under blacksmiths like Bill Morton and Jock Holliday. In 1966, Mr. Albert Taylor was given a presentation to mark fifty years service with the firm. Mr. Ernie Alderson and Mr. Frank Pennington were foremen then, and Mr. Taylor's son Raymond, a co. director. The firm closed in the early 1970s, when all the workshops were bought by Armstrong Massey, who eventually sold the original workshops to Comet Ltd.[13]

Life at the John Bull

Mrs. Davies remembered all the lively times that were had at the John Bull when her parents took over the licence in the 1930s. Her grandmother Mrs. K. Waite had a shop next to the John Bull selling papers and groceries. After the death of the landlord, Mr. Batters, her parents took over both businesses, the pub and the shop. A Mr. C. Mercer eventually moved into the shop and they just had the pub. Mr. Waite was a very amiable man and well liked in the area. He had a good trade, in spite of the fact that in the 1930s some of the houses in the small streets near the Foss were being demolished and people were moving from the district. The John Bull was the focal point of the area and young lads could hardly wait to come of age to drink with their fathers.

John Bull before 1937. *Courtesy of Y.E.P.*   John Bull after 1937. *Courtesy of Y.E.P.*

The new John Bull was opened in 1937, the old pub never being closed while the alterations took place. Huge tarpaulins were draped over the front of the building whilst the new leaded windows were put in place. (Mock Tudor styled front). The new pub was as successful as the old. It boasted a good darts team, which won many trophies over the years. Customers looked forward to their domino school and interesting conversations. At the weekend there was Jack Mercer on the piano and Joe Langdon as Master of Ceremonies, as customers got up to do their "turns". This was always followed by a good singsong with everyone joining in.

Mrs. Davies remembered her mother opening the doors at the front and back simultaneously, and shouting "Now" so customers who were queuing up outside could pour into the lounge at the same time. Every seat was taken in the first minute. Once it was said the Reverend Bainton had bemoaned that he wished people would queue for his church, St. Cuthbert's, as readily. On Mondays they used to have a "Monday Night at Eight", which was a talent show, when everyone got up and did a "turn". There were always some very good trips to the seaside. The men's and lady's trips were separate, and always on a different day, so they could all let themselves "go" without any awkward questions being asked.

There was always something happening. Frank Herbert or "Yank" as he was called, used to help Mr. Waite by filling shelves and was a prime target for a joke. Once he was kidded into boxing Jimmy O' Brian, and a ring was duly made at the bottom of the yard near the river, all the spectators raged around cheering and shouting. Before they had actually started boxing unknown to him "Yank's" gloves were smeared with something red, and every time he landed a blow Jimmy looked as though he was "bleeding". They boxed and boxed, "Yank" being assured he was winning by the amount of blood all over Jimmy. When they were both exhausted, "Yank" was declared the winner, but it remained a topic of discussion for a long time. Later in the war, "Yank" was one of the first to be called up, and took part in the Normandy landings.

At closing time one night, someone suggested having a diving competition off Layerthorpe Bridge, with Sep Aspinall as judge. Despite objections from wives and girl friends, five or six men in their underpants stood on the bridge and at the count of three had to dive. Bull Kirby, the local strong man was the only one to dive the others got dressed. Poor Bull came out of the river dripping wet and cussing, but he won a few pints that night. The same Bull was once helping Mr. Waite and George Warriner to move a piano up the iron staircase at the back of the house. They were at one end and Bull at the other end and he complained bitterly that if only he

Inside the John Bull before closure in 1994. The interior remained unchanged from the 1930s.
Courtesy of Y.E.P.

had a man at the other end it would be a lot easier. Mr. Waite and George were too exhausted even to feel insulted. One Sunday, after the pub had closed for lunch a group of customers went down Skin Yard which was near the pub and led to the rear entrance, to play pitch and toss (very illegal in those days). A few minutes later the police came running down the yard to try and catch the men, it was bedlam with everyone running around. Ronnie Long climbed over two walls and helped a very surprised Mr. Holmes, who had a shop two doors away, to sharpen tools on his large stone wheel. Four or five men ran to the river and tried to climb along the back of Skin Yard over the River Foss to escape. The most ingenious of all the gang, Arnie Clark, came into Mrs. Waite's kitchen and pretended he was having his dinner with them.

Mrs. Davies remembered too, how the pub which was near the river would often flood and how the fire brigade had to pump the water out of the cellars. She said it was often difficult getting things back to normal after the floods. After one bad flood in 1942 the water was up to a couple of feet inside the pub, and people had to walk on trestles on the roads outside.[14]

Characters

In the 1930s and 40s there were many local "characters" in the area. Mick Metcalf was the local rag and boneman, who lived in Hallfield Road. He had a wooden leg, a stump with no joint and a rubber cup at the base, possibly a victim of the Boer war. He operated with a pony and cart, which he kept in the out-buildings behind the house of Mr. Laverack, on the corner of Layerthorpe and Duke of York Street. Christopher "Kit" or "Bull" Kirby lived at 4 Morley Street. He had been to sea and his strength was considerable. He was reputed to be able to lift an old cast iron mangle on to a cart unaided.

John Thomas Giles Peacock, known to all as Jockey Giles, lived at the bottom of Downhill Street. In the 1930s, he had been involved in whippet racing on a track in Osbaldwick lane. For many years he was a coal and firewood merchant, and during the war when coal was rationed, he was reputed always to be able to get additional supplies. Jockey Giles was a very colourful character, he often wore western gear and one of his cars he drove was a pink Vauxhall Cresta. He had a finger in many "pies" and always planned to "make a million". He wanted to cross an alsatian with a greyhound and breed a new type of dog an "Also Grey". He talked of building a roller skating rink near "Ossies" yard. He often employed children to work for him, and bought them fish & chips instead of wages. He was good hearted and always lent his horse and cart for bonfire night collections. In later years he and his wife had a betting shop at the corner of Downhill Street. Mr. A. Camidge also remembered a Mr. Ted Ellison, who went round the pubs selling his cockles and mussels.

Tommy Mason was the cycle repair man with a shop in Layerthorpe at the corner of Chicory Yard. Mr. D Poole remembered him charging one shilling to mend a puncture in the 1950s.

The fish and chip shop at 67 Layerthorpe, was run by a Welshman, David Rees (Dai) Prosser, very well known as an outstanding rugby league forward with both Leeds and York, from about 1931. Another Welshman who had joined York about the same time as Prosser, Horace Coldrick, was the landlord of the Frog Hall Inn for many years after the war. These two had married two local girls who were close friends, Helena Holmes and Ann Gibson. Tragically both ladies died within two years of each other about 1960 aged about 50.

A man who lived for many years on the front of Layerthorpe, just to the west of the junction with Redeness Street, was Martin Durkin, who was born in Hungate. He celebrated his 103rd. birthday in Glen Lodge, where he lived for the last few years of his life. He died in February 1993.

Two more people who will always be remembered with affection by ex-Layerthorpe people were PC. Kidney the resident policeman of the 1930s and the Rev. Pyne the Rector of St Cuthbert's (1910-1934). All Layerthorpe turned out for the funeral of this rector. He was loved by all the local inhabitants, and his familiar figure, riding up and down Layerthorpe from his vicarage home at the bottom of Heworth Village to St. Cuthbert's Church on his bicycle giving rides to all the children will always be remembered.[15]

King George V Silver Jubilee 1935. Residents of Richmond, Bateson, Little Hallfield Road and Webster Street.   *Courtesy of Bill Dickenson*

Chapter VII. Notes and References

(1) Information supplied by Mrs. A. Barton, 68 Fordlands Road.
(2) *Kelly's* 1907, 1920, 1930.
(3) Information supplied by Mrs. Finch, 13 Elmlands Grove.
(4) Information supplied by Mrs. Poole, 6 Horsman Avenue.
(5) Information supplied by Mr. Camidge.
(6) *Kelly's* 1920, 1930.
(7) Information supplied by Mrs. Johnson, 21 Thirkleby Way, Mrs. M. White, 8 Cranbrook Avenue and Mrs. O. King, 147 Bishopthorpe Road.
(8) Information supplied by Mrs. Hale, 86 Knighthorpe Road, Loughborough.
(9) Information supplied by Mrs. Wakelin, 4 Larchfields.
(10) Information supplied by Mr. & Mrs. Cole, 16 Walney Road.
(11) Information supplied by Mrs. O. King.
(12) York Gas Company, *Centenary of Gas Lighting,* 1824-1924. Ben Johnson
(13) Information supplied by Mr. R. Taylor. Mrs. M. Taylor, 23 Millfield Lane.
(14) Information supplied by Mrs. S. Davies, 14 Mill Lane.
(15) Information supplied by Mr. Poole, Mr. Camidge, Miss. P. Coldrick.

CHAPTER VIII

Second World War and After

In 1939 at the start of the Second World War, eleven A.R.P. wardens took over the babies cloakroom in Bilton Street School as an A.R.P. station. In September 1939, when War was declared the school was closed, and the children given homework. Some pupils started to go to school part time, but the school wasn't fully re opened until January 1940. The teachers took turns to do fire duty at the school.

In April 1942 in the Baedaker raid on York a bomb dropped in Mansfield Street destroying three houses. The main classroom at Bilton Street school was damaged, and two outer doors were blown off their hinges and upstairs twenty windows were broken. Lessons were often interrupted by sirens. In another raid in York on the 18th. of December 1942 a bomb was dropped in the school yard, there were no casualties but it left a large crater. On another occasion a bomb landed near the gas works which damaged the Co-op and nearby houses.

On V.E. day the school had two days holiday. In 1946 Miss. A. Story was the headmistress. The school was closed in 1956, when Mrs. B.M. Pearce was the last headmistress, the official closing ceremony being on the 16th. July. Parents were invited to a final service and the children were presented with leaving certificates.[1]

Frog Hall, circa 1930. Showing Skinner's newsagents and Greenwood's hairdressers.
Courtesy of Y.E.P.

Life at the Frog Hall

The Frog Hall was essentially a man's public house. It was advertised in an advertising calendar as "where sportsmen meet". The licence was held by Horace Coldrick, from 1949 to 1973. He was a York rugby league player before the war.

In 1949 Layerthorpe was densely populated. The public houses were the Frog Hall, George IV and the John Bull. The George IV had a licence only to sell beer and was very small. The Frog Hall had a "men only" bar, (which existed until the next landlord took over in 1973) smoke room, lounge (known as the singing room) and a passage.

In the early 1950s many older women would come into the passage for a drink and take draught beer home with them in a jug, especially on a Sunday morning, to drink whilst cooking the dinner. During those years the singing room was very popular on Saturday nights, and was used by both sexes. The smoke room was rarely used. Darts and dominoes were very popular, darts being very competitive with an "A" and "B" team in the league.

In the early years Jockey Giles organised many activities from the Frog Hall. There were fancy dress walking matches and pram races on his land (now the site of Netto). He was also the chairman of "The Shaving Club". On Sunday mornings men would come to the "Frog" for inspection, some clean shaved, some unshaved and some with false beards. The chairman imposed fines according to the state of the whiskers or for insolence if they answered back or for dumb insolence if they didn't. The money raised was put towards outings for customers. Additional money was raised from Saturday night raffles. Outings were always for single sex. Men would have a day at the seaside, women an outing to a Leeds pantomime and a fish and chip tea or evening meal at a country public house. Because of sporting interest, especially Rugby League, a separately financed outing to the Rugby League final at Wembley was an annual event.

There was a great community spirit among the customers, who were always willing to help out in an emergency, bringing up bottles from the cellar at busy times. Even after the demolition of most of the houses in the sixties, many who had moved away to live in Tang Hall, still remained loyal customers.

There was always a great affinity with the Boys' Club in Layerthorpe. The leader for many years was a Scotsman known as "Skipper". He was a regular customer and the "Frog" sponsored some of the club's sports events. Boys were allowed to leave their bicycles down the "Frogs" yard.

Once the houses in Layerthorpe were demolished trade declined, but the "Frog" still managed to run a darts team and organise its annual trips. The singing room came to life again in the 1960s when a juke box was installed and attracted younger people from Tang Hall.

A pensioners party became an annual event each January. All customers past and present over the age of sixty five were invited to a supper and entertainment. They were also given a bag of fruit and a small amount of cash to take home. The first one was opened officially by the local councillor, chemist Jack Wood, who started the ball rolling for the next year with a donation.[2]

The Rope Walk

The Rope Walk was situated in a field adjacent to Kidd's Terrace. There had been a mention of a Rope Walk and rope makers in Layerthorpe since Victorian times.[3] In the 1950s it was owned by the Shambles Rope Shop, whose employees at regular intervals used to make ropes of various dimensions. There were huts at either end of the field between which strands of twine were strung out. Gearing wheels in each hut then twisted the strands into the required rope thickness.[4]

York Boys' Club

This club originated in Hungate in the 1930s and was forced to move to Layerthorpe after demolition orders. It was situated in Redeness Street, in the building which had formerly been the Layerthorpe Adult School. The ground floor had a gymnasium, an office, bathroom and shower. On the upper floor was the games room, canteen, meeting room and showers. The club was affiliated to the National Association of Boys' Clubs and had a full time leader, and part time supervisors of woodwork, art, gymnastics and drama. The leader in the 1950s was William Ogilvie, always known to members as "Skip". He had replaced Chris Harrison who had left in 1949 after seventeen years of service. The club had thriving football, cricket and table tennis teams, and entered productions in the annual Youth Drama Festival every year. Summer weekend camps were organised at Naburn Hall by the kind permission of Commander George Palmes who allowed the club to camp in his fields. A fortnight camp was arranged every year in the south of England, where valuable lessons were learnt in discipline and tidy living. "Skip" died suddenly in December 1957 and the era of the full time leader was at an end. His replacement was Gordon Goddard, a long time voluntary worker at the club, who was to give many years of devoted service, culminating in the award of the B.E.M. in 1980, having won the highest N.A.B.C. award, the silver keystone, in 1979.

Coronation Party, 6th June 1953

Foss Islands Road 1959. Showing laundry and laundry house.

Layerthorpe main road 1959.

In the early 1960s the Layerthorpe area was demolished and redeveloped and the club moved to 84 Lowther Street where it is still in operation. During the 1940s the army cadet force was attached to the Boys' Club, where they held their weapons. Later they had their own army cadet hut in Little Hallfield Road.[5]

Demolition

In 1959 and 1960 compulsory purchase orders were made by York City Council for most of the houses left in Layerthorpe. Bilton Street and Redeness Street and the area near Hallfield road, were some of the first areas to be demolished. After the houses were demolished on one side of Layerthorpe, the road at that side was widened. The whole process took a number of years to accomplish as there were so many owners of one or two houses. Each owner was notified and a price given for his property. Each tenant was assessed and offered alternative suitable accommodation, as far as possible to suit individual needs. Unlike the 1930's demolition, when all tenants were moved to a certain area, the tenants of these years were re-housed in different parts of the city.[6]

On the other side of the street, which contained the Frog Hall and John Bull, the houses and small shops did not come down until much later. Indeed some shops still traded until the 1980s and 1990s.

After the houses in Hart's Terrace and Wilson's Terrace had gone, Gladstone's Garage and Gladstone's Tyre and Battery Distributions were opened. Mr. John Lewis Laverack was the chairman of Gladstone's Garage and lived at Gladstone House, which stood at the corner of Hawthorne Street and Layerthorpe. He was the grandson of Matthew Laverack, a coal merchant in Layerthorpe in the early 1900s. John Lewis Laverack was elected the Conservative candidate for the Heworth ward 1973-1982, being sheriff of York in 1978. He was a member of a large family of Laveracks who had lived and worked in Layerthorpe from the early part of this century.[7]

The Derwent Valley Industrial Estate was established in the 1970s in the area where the old railway station and coal yards had been. The train lines were taken up in the 1990s and a cycle track was made by Sustrans, which runs from Osbaldwick to Wigginton Road past Rowntree's factory.

W. Avery weighing machine manufacturers, York Motor Factors and Armstrong Massey car dealers occupied the area where the entrances to Bilton Street and Redeness Street had been. Taylor's Engineering works were closed in the 1970s and Comet Ltd built on that site. Allied Carpets Ltd were opened in the area where the laundry and laundry house had been.

Right side.

12 Craven M. A. & Son Ltd.
  (joiners' shop)
14 Asher Mrs
16 Cookland Hubert
18 **Paxton** Mrs
20 Long Ernest
22 Lancaster Frank A
York Incorporated (Church
  of England) Sunday
  School Committee
Taylor C. J. & Son Ltd.
  genl. engnrs

LAYERTHORPE.

Layerthorpe bridge to Haw
thorn grove.

Left side.

Walker J. H. & Co. (York)
  Ltd. builders' mers. &
  coal mers. T N 22051,
  53874 & 22233
7 Holmes Mrs. Jane A
9 Mercer C. G. newsagt
11 John Bull Inn
15 Botterill W. R. fruitr
Hossell J. J. & H. (York)
  Ltd. fellmongers
21/27 Stirks   Furnishing
  Stores, house furnishers
...... here is Chicory yard .....
31 Mason Thos. cycle agt
33 Booth Miss Ada
33 Silcock Mrs. Ida, shopkpr
39 Lila's, wool store
41 (flat 1) Abbott Thos
43 Gladstone Garage (York)
  Ltd. motor engnrs
45 Wilson Wm
45 Wilson Mrs. Jane Ann,
  secondhand clothes dlr
47 & 49 Jock's   Hairdressing
  Salon
49 Ferris Thos
53 Cammidge Albt. W
55 Makin Mrs. M. grocer
57 Barnett Mrs. M
...... here is Downhill st ....
61 Clark Jn. J. shopkpr
63 Costello Thos
65 Whiting D. & N. grocers
67 Prossers Fisheries, fried
  fish dlrs
69 Cassins R. W. butcher
73 Holmes Harry
75 Craven Mrs. Annie H. fruitr
..... here is Wilson's yard ......
83 Nicholson Fredk
83 Depasquale Carmelo, boot
  & shoe dlr
85 Audin Jn. H. butcher
87 Frog Hall Inn
91 Bowen Douglas
91 Greenwood E. F. hairdrssr
107 Jefferson Rd
109 Douglas Jn. P
111 Smith Mrs. Elsie
113 Kent Ernest
115 Thackway Jas
117 Ellison Miss Eliza
119 Parker Geo. J
121 Foster Jsph. W
123 Stonehouse Ernest T
125 Walker Geo. D
127 Wrigglesworth Tom
129 Dickenson Alfd

30 Pearson Laurence
34 Walsh Mrs. E
36 Hume Mrs
38 Utley Sidney
40 Pearce Frank
42 Milner   Mrs.   Charlotte,
  shopkpr
44 Lyth Mrs
46 Hick Mrs
48 Harrison Chas
50 Metcalfe Mrs
.... here is Bilton st ....
54 Wilkinson Jas. M
56 Williams Herbt
58 Durkin Martin
62 Key Harry, shopkpr
.........here is Redeness st.........
64 Coates Ernest
66 Hardaker Mrs. Stella
68 Peacock David
70 Redhead Jas. L
72 Hare Thos. B
74 Linfoot Tom
76/78 York Co-operative Society Ltd
.. here are St. Cuthbert's &
  Hallfield roads ...
80 Evans Mrs. Kate
82 Freeman Thos. G
84 Laverick Fredk
86 Husband Anthony
88 Cochrane Geo. W
90 Kent Mrs. Florence
92 Watson Wm
94 Watson S. grocer
Gladstone Motors (show-
  rooms)
... here is Duke of York st ...
106 Pask Jsph. W
108 Thompson Jsph
110 Thompson Kenneth
112 Harrison Arth. L
112 (rear of) Harrison Arth.
  L. motor garage
114 Kelsall D. & I. grocers
116 Ross Wm. O., B.Sc
118 Thompson Miss Emily
120 & 122 Smith A. & F. ladies'
  outfitters
122 Smith Miss Annie
124 Hunter Mrs. Dorothy
126 Fletcher Miss Violet
130 Bell Tom
132 Godson Leonard
134 Dixon Mrs. Annie

Reproduced from Kellys Street Directory 1959. *Courtesy of Kellys*

On the other side of the road, Walkers remained at their Foss Bank site until 1973, when they moved further down Foss Islands Road. Their old offices were taken over by Laverack Builders, then Stonelands Construction Ltd, then Hirepoint, now all the old buildings are demolished. R&P Turnbull and Armstrong Massey car dealers had moved into the site where previously Stirk's Furniture Stores had been.[8] The John Bull public house was demolished in 1995 and the land taken over by extensions to Turnbull's garage and car show rooms. York Auto Spares remained near Wilson's Yard until 1995. This area is now the site of the new Netto Supermarket opened in November 1995. The Frog Hall public house still remains, but new houses and luxury flats have been built in the area where Vicar's Row and Vicar's Terrace once stood. Little remains now to remind us of the many houses, yards, shops and small businesses that was "old" Layerthorpe.

Chapter VIII Notes and References

(1) Y.C.A. *Bilton Street School log books* (1939-1956).

(2) Information supplied by Miss. P. Coldrick.

(3) *Kellys*. (1880-1900).

(4) Information supplied by Mr. D. Poole.

(5) Ibid.

(6) Y.C.A. *Compulsory Purchase Orders, Layerthorpe* (1959-1960).

(7) Y.R.L. Murray, H, *Pedigrees of York Families*. Y 929 . 2.

(8) *Kellys*. (1960-1975).

Summary and Conclusion

Layerthorpe began as a small Viking settlement. In medieval times it had its own church and was in a separate parish, St. Mary's. The people were quite poor then and the village did not start to grow until after the Industrial Revolution. When the railways and engineering works were begun in the York area there was a great demand for more houses.

A few gentry and middle class people were among some of the first to move into the new houses built in Bilton Street and Redeness Street. An article in the Yorkshire Gazette in 1831 advertised eleven houses for sale in Bilton Street, described as well built and in an area greatly improving.

Unfortunately, because of the drainage and sewerage problems and bad roads, the area did not improve much in the next hundred years. More houses were built for working class men in a confined area. Some of these new houses were back to back and very shut in, with inadequate sanitation. As more of these substandard houses were built, most of the gentry and middle class inhabitants moved out to Heworth and Clifton, leaving Layerthorpe a predominantly working class area.

In Victorian and Edwardian times, there was a lot of overcrowding in Layerthorpe and much poverty and sickness. It was a poor area, with many labourers, skilled and semi-skilled tradesmen earning insufficient wages to keep their large families. After the First World War, steps were taken to try and improve the area. After some of the older houses near the Foss were demolished and the tenants moved to new houses in Pottery Lane and Dodsworth Avenue, the remaining area was declared an improvement area. Most of the remaining houses were modernised and the whole area became a much healthier place to live in.

After the demolition of most of the houses in the 1960s the area became an industrial estate. There is now only one public house, the Frog Hall and only one branch of the family of Horwell's coal merchants, still operating from their premises in Mansfield Street. A few houses in Faber Street and Hallfield Road, and one cafe, "Hungry Horace", formerly Arthur Savory's cafe on the main Layerthorpe road, remain. The only signs of the busy, crowded area that was Layerthorpe. This year, 1996, Layerthorpe Bridge is being altered once again, and a new bridge built over the Foss near Walker's old coal yard. The construction of these new bridges will completely alter the appearance of Foss Bank.

However, many people re-housed or moved away remember their days in Layerthorpe with nostalgia and affection. Although it was a poor area and in spite of its problems most of its inhabitants strove to be clean and respectable. White steps and white pinnys were most prized and respectability was the key word.

There was always a great sense of community, now alas gone from many modern areas. And as one lady recalled, "there was always a neighbour to help, someone to turn to in times of trouble, but also many happy days to remember".

A.E.Webster

1996

T H E   A U T H O R

Avril Webster was born in Hull but evacuated to York at the start of World War Two. In 1942 she came with her parents to live in Heworth, where she has lived for most of her life. Educated at Tang Hall School and Mill Mount Grammar School she joined the staff at York City Library in 1949 to train as a librarian. A keen local historian she was a contributor to the book on the history of Osbaldwick Village published in 1981. In 1987 she gained a Certificate of Local History from York University and used her interest and knowledge in that subject to research into other areas in North Yorkshire. She has written articles and organised many local history displays. In 1994 she retired from the library service after 28 years of being in charge of Osbaldwick Village Library. In recent years she has researched and given talks on Layerthorpe and the Heworth area, places she has known since childhood. Although she now spends the winter months abroad she still enjoys researching and writing about areas in and around her favourite city, York.

INDEX OF PEOPLE AND PLACES